VIRGINIA'S
CIVIL RIGHTS
HERO
CURTIS W. HARRIS SR.

WILLIAM PAUL LAZARUS

THE
History
PRESS

Published by The History Press
Charleston, SC
www.historypress.com

Front cover: The Reverend Curtis W. Harris Sr. leads a 1982 protest in Petersburg, Virginia. *Used with permission from the Valentine Corporation.*

First published 2023

Manufactured in the United States

ISBN 9781467153249

Library of Congress Control Number: 2022944980

This book is dedicated to the many heroes of the Civil Rights Movement. A few became famous. Some were killed or injured. Many were forgotten. Others, like Rev. Curtis W. Harris Sr., were more active on the local and statewide level, where their efforts created the base that allowed the national work to endure and, finally, begin eroding centuries of ingrained racism.

CONTENTS

ACKNOWLEDGEMENTS

A special thanks to Jeremy M. Lazarus, who proposed this book and took photographs, and to my editors, Jon Swebilius and Deb Eskite. I also want to thank Anne Johnson from the College of William & Mary Library; Felicia Irving from Carter Woodson School in Hopewell and Jeanie Langford from the Appomattox Regional Library System; the Dendron Historical Society; and Andrew Shannon from the Southern Christian Leadership Conference. I especially want to acknowledge Dr. Lauranett Lorraine Lee, who collected a series of oral interviews from Hopewell residents for her book *Making the American Dream Work: A Cultural History of African Americans in Hopewell, Virginia*, as well as a variety of other researchers who guaranteed that the voices of the men and women who fought America's intense racism will live forever.

INTRODUCTION

Today, African Americans increasingly belong to an ever-growing middle class in the United States. Overall, more than 20 percent of Blacks in this country are managers or professionals. That's four times the total from fifty years ago. Other statistics reflect the increasing success of Blacks in this country. In the late 1990s, before the economic downturn in 2007, Black poverty rates hit 23 percent, then a record low. In 2018, the rate declined to 21.2 percent. At the same time, in March 2018, Black unemployment reached a new low of 6.6 percent, continuing a descent that started five years earlier.

In 2020, the Congressional Joint Economic Committee released its study, *The Economic State of Black America in 2020*, and found that

> *America made significant progress in reducing social and economic disparities in the latter half of the 20th century, as discriminatory policies like segregation, redlining, employment discrimination and restricted voting rights were outlawed. Black Americans have achieved success in many visible fields, from sports and entertainment to politics. That said, there are still deep inequities across social and economic indicators that will take awareness and concerted effort to address.*
>
> *Black Americans have made more progress in the 21st century in reducing gaps in educational attainment than in other areas. At the secondary level, the shares of Black and White young adults who have dropped out are falling and converging, while the shares of Black and White adults with*

high school diplomas or GEDs are rising and converging. Black Americans
have made progress in attaining postsecondary education as well, doubling
the share of Black college graduates since 1990.

There are still important areas of disparity, including income and economic opportunities. A 2022 report by the National Urban League found that "Black people still get only 73.9 percent of the American pie white people enjoy." Overall, the Equality Index found that "while Black people have made economic and health gains, they've slipped further behind white people in education, social justice and civic engagement since this index was launched in 2005."

Nevertheless, the gap between the Black and white population is narrowing, reflecting changing racial attitudes. A 2001 study by the Kaiser Family Foundation revealed that whites have more contact and closer relationships with their Black counterparts than thirty-five or forty years ago. Those numbers have continued to improve. Whites increasingly agree with their Black counterparts on multiple issues, including equal employment and intermarriage.

Proximity has changed attitudes. A 2019 study by the *Washington Post* found that a majority of white respondents thought the government is obligated to ensure that minorities have access to schools that are equal in quality to majority-white schools, equal access to health care and equality in the courts. More than half said they didn't care about the race of their spouse. The vast majority didn't care about the race of an adopted child. And 61 percent of Black participants said they lived in integrated neighborhoods.

In contrast, back in the 1950s, according to the study, 44 percent of whites said they "might or definitely would move if a Black person became their next-door neighbor." By 1997, that percentage had dropped to 1 percent. In 1961, only 50 percent of the population said they would vote for a Black presidential candidate. Some thirty-seven years later, 79 percent of voters said they would. In 2008 and 2012, the majority in this country did exactly that.

The authors noted the results of the survey were very consistent: "More tolerance, less racism."

No one could have imagined this happening when Curtis West Harris was born in Dendron, Virginia, in 1924. Just three months before, the Virginia state legislature passed the Racial Integrity Act, which banned interracial marriage down to "a single drop" of African blood. Harris was the sixth child of an impoverished sharecropper and his wife, living in a desolate outpost of the commonwealth while the sweeping regulation was passed by the most prominent men in the state. In time, however, Harris would lead the fight against this law and many others designed to maintain the white majority's control over minorities in Virginia and in the rest of the South.

Eventually, Harris's efforts combined with the work of many others nationally would help reverse centuries of racial discrimination that began when slaves first arrived in Virginia in 1619. His determination in the face of intense hostility took him to the forefront of America's Civil Rights Movement, arm in arm with the Reverend Martin Luther King Jr. By the end of his career, Rev. Harris was widely recognized as a monument to freedom on the local, state and national levels.

The Reverend Curtis W. Harris Sr. *Courtesy of Appomattox Regional Library System, Petersburg, Virginia.*

Most of the other giants of civil rights passed on before him: King, Ralph Abernathy, Whitney Young, Rosa Parks and so many more. Virtually all left detailed accounts of their lives to inspire and motivate those who were to follow. Rev. Harris had never done that. He had always been reluctant to talk about the past.

"It was," he would invariably say when asked, "a long time ago."

Several years ago, beset by illness, he decided the time had come to recall the years of sit-ins and marches, the confrontations and the quiet determination to bring an end to the long years of injustice.

Unfortunately, Rev. Harris died in 2017, before this book could be completed. His story, however, remains poignant and important.

CHAPTER 1

EARLY LIFE

COMMUNITY HISTORY, SCHOOLING

The Reverend Curtis W. Harris's earliest memories went back to 1928, when he was barely four years old, living in Dendron, Virginia, a tiny community tucked into the corner of Surry County. It had three thousand residents in the 1920s. Today, the population is closer to three hundred.

The area has changed little in the intervening years. Located across the James River from Colonial Williamsburg in what is called the Hampton Roads area, Surry still barely qualifies as a metropolitan area. The population of the entire county was little more than seven thousand people in 2010. Then, as now, residents derived their income from hog farming and lumber. That started in 1609, when the first English settlers erected Smith's Fort on Gray's Creek. They also built a fort on nearby Hog Island, which thrived— as its name implies—as a place to raise pigs. Corn, soybeans and peanuts still flourish in the county's rich soil. Livestock continue to graze placidly in the fields, just as the animals have there for three hundred years.

Occasionally, major events would illuminate the area. In 1622, 347 settlers died in an Indian massacre. Later, residents marched in the Confederate army under their own banners: the Surry Cavalry and the Surry Light Artillery. After that, the county reverted to its bucolic, backwater status. A few years before Harris was born, Surry—named for an English county—flourished briefly as a lumber center. The community depended on the success of a single industry, headed by the Surry Lumber Company. Eventually, the firm became the largest producer of yellow pine lumber in the eastern United

States, but production topped out around 1920 as local supplies dwindled and competition increased.

Harris's family did not share in the local prosperity. His father, Sandy, was a sharecropper, the common fate of the descendants of former slaves who had no place to go after the Civil War. Harris's great-grandparents had been freed but stayed on the land they had once worked as slaves. Many others did, too, either forced by coercion or because of their limited skills. Harris's father was among those who remained. The family barely scraped by, one of many Black southern families deeply embedded in poverty.

The railroad track ran next to the Harris home. Six days a week, a Surry, Sussex and Southampton Railway locomotive would chug past, carrying railcars filled with logs harvested by lumberjacks based in nearby camps. The train had special significance to the Harris family. Shortly before Harris was born, his father gave up on farming and began taking the railroad to Richmond in hopes of finding work. He would hitch a ride home on the caboose, raising a white rag to signal his children upon his return.

Days after Harris was born, his father was supposed to come back from his weekly foray to the state capital, located about sixty miles away. "My mother was in the bed, and she could see the train, too," Harris said, relating a family tale. "She was holding me up, so I could see the train. My brothers and sisters were outside to wave at the train. When it got to the end of the train, (my father) was not there." The other five children waited for the next train, but their father wasn't on that one, either. Eventually, Harris's mother told the children to stop waiting.

Thelma Harris never talked about her husband again. Perhaps she had expected him to disappear one day. That often happened in Black families. After the Civil War ended slavery, African American families stagnated because limited jobs and education undermined their feelings of self-worth. Women, seen mostly in the role of mothers, found they had to take over both financially and emotionally as men struggled to succeed in a hostile environment. For many Black women, this was simply a continuation of slave conditions. During the time of slavery, deprived of the right to marry or even to retain their children, Black women had grown accustomed to having children outside of marriage. They were used to being single parents, regardless of the hardships that implied.

Harris did not see his father until twelve years later and then only briefly. Inexplicably and unannounced, Sandy dropped in to complain that his wife was not doing a good job raising the children and then left Harris's life forever.

Eventually, the family could not afford to stay in Dendron—whose name, ironically, was derived from the Greek word for "trees." It had originally been called Mussel Fork Village but was renamed in 1896. The U.S. economy was growing; the future looked brighter most everywhere except in Harris's hometown. As headquarters of the lumber company, Dendron once featured "two banks, a movie theater, several schools, two bakeries, many churches, an automobile dealership and about 20 stores," according to an essay by Jack Huber published in the winter 2000 edition of *Virginia Trees*. In 1920, two thousand people called the community home, enjoying the electricity supplied by the company and the ice plant.

By 1925, however, most of the readily available pine trees had been cut down. The lumber company tottered along. At one time, three sawmills ground out an estimated four hundred thousand board feet a day. Eventually, workers often showed up for their shift only to find the gates locked. The lumber mills finally closed permanently in October 1927, some forty years after they sliced up their first logs. The railroad stopped its regular runs past the Harris home. Surry Lumber owned much of the town and dismantled almost everything after closing. As a result, by 1930, Dendron had lost its water system and electricity along with its sole employer.

Harris recalled a fire that also hastened the economic collapse, although newspaper files indicate the only major Dendron fire of the era occurred in 1931, several years after the family left.

With the mill now history, residents of Dendron and nearby Sedley, Vicksville and Central Hill started exiting in droves, looking for jobs anywhere else. With no public assistance programs, wage earners had no choice. Within a few years, multiple Dendron homes were deserted. Streets were empty. An estimated 80 percent of the residents abandoned the city and moved on. For the few residents left, the top employer these days is the Surry County public schools.

In 1928, Harris and his family joined the refugees. The family packed up their meager belongings and moved to nearby Hopewell, about thirty-five miles north. Located where the Appomattox and James Rivers meet, it was another historic region with its own ties to the earliest years of English settlement. In 1613, Sir Thomas Dale settled this area on a bluff overlooking the two rivers, just six years after the founding of Jamestown, the first European community in Virginia, named for James I of England. The town was then called Bermuda City. It later became Charles City Point and, finally, City Point. It didn't survive long; Indians overran it in 1622. Hopewell was reestablished in 1635 and named for the ship that brought the founding family, the Eppes, across the Atlantic Ocean, although the City Point name lingered on. Eventually, more than two hundred years later, the city of Hopewell grew around the old settlement and annexed City Point.

The area briefly enjoyed some limelight centuries after its founding. General Ulysses S. Grant set up his headquarters in Hopewell late in the Civil War and oversaw the ten-month siege of Petersburg from there. Simultaneously, City Point turned into one of busiest seaports in the world as supplies were delivered there for the Union army. President Abraham Lincoln stopped by for a visit in 1864 and again in 1865. When the war ended, farming resumed its role as the economic mainstay for the next fifty years.

The economy picked up just prior to World War I, less than two decades before the Harris family trudged into town. In 1912, engineers from E.I. DuPont de Nemours decided the area would be perfect for a new dynamite plant because of the port and access to railroads. Then, only an estimated three hundred people lived in Hopewell. That would change quickly. The company purchased land from nearby Hopewell Farms and spent two years building a plant. Business really picked up in 1914 with the start of World War I. DuPont eventually employed thirty thousand people in Hopewell and daily produced more than one million pounds of guncotton, which is used to make smokeless gunpowder.

"It very quickly turned into the largest guncotton factory in the world," said Jeanie Langford, archivist at the Appomattox Regional Library. "It's been said that Hopewell saved Europe."

Hopewell quickly divided into Black and white sections. Armed with a contract with England to supply dynamite for the Great War, DuPont needed to build houses as quickly and cheaply as possible. Aladdin Homes of Bay City, Michigan, provided precut kits for different styles of homes in four separate villages: A Village in City Point for management and technical workers; B Village for white workers; South B Village for African Americans; and Southwest B Village for immigrant workers. Houses typically contained five or six rooms with a columned porch in front.

In 1915, the city's downtown was virtually razed by a fire, which incinerated three hundred buildings and caused an estimated $2 million in damages. No one was killed by the fire, which started in a three-frame building on Appomattox Street then occupied by a restaurant. A teenager spotted the fire and had to be rescued along with his infant sibling.

Residents initially called for military help in case spies had caused the fire, a natural fear given the United States was moving closer to joining the war raging in Europe. Newspaper accounts include the arrest of a German "spy" who was found inside the DuPont plant with maps and blueprints of the plant in his pockets. He was supposedly trying to ignite chemicals to burn down guncotton awaiting shipment. No follow-up story appeared. On the other hand, one local resident didn't survive the destruction.

According to a *New York Times* report, "Citizens of the town just after nightfall detected a negro [*sic*] in the act of looting. He was hanged….The negro [*sic*] was found carrying off clothing from a pile in front of a burning store. He was seized at once by a party of citizens and hurried into a side street. After a moment's consultation a rope was placed about his neck and he was hanged from a tree."

Fortunately for the city, the dynamite plant escaped the blaze. DuPont turned down offers for help, including one from John Ringling of Ringling Brothers Circus to send men and elephants, and rebuilt the city. The subsequent reconstruction of the town fueled the local economy and more growth. This time, the city opted for more durable brick structures, many of which have survived.

Hopewell boomed under DuPont, which imported many European workers. The workforce reached forty thousand people. The *New York Times* called Hopewell the "Wonder City…a town of mushroom growth." Imported workers spoke an estimated twenty-three languages. The community was incorporated without going through the usual bureaucratic process. The state legislature responded by passing a law to prevent instant towns from springing up in the future.

The mixture of residents was volatile, particularly in an era when race riots began to dot the American landscape as impoverished Blacks began migrating north to compete with whites for jobs in the burgeoning factories there. They were joined by soldiers being demobilized as World War I slowed and then ended, creating a lethal mixture. On July 1, 1917, the confluence led to a deadly riot in East St. Louis after a Black man supposedly killed a white man. During the week of intermittent fighting, nine white residents and hundreds of African Americans were killed.

The unrest spread nationwide, even to distant Hopewell. In October 1918, a Black female laborer at the DuPont plant got into some sort of fight with a white male supervisor, Gomez. The *Hopewell Record* reported that "the trouble broke out at 2 o'clock yesterday when…Gomez…discharged a negress [*sic*] from the mess hall, and in the argument ensuring is alleged to have slapped her." The *Richmond Times-Dispatch* recorded: "The row begun shortly after 2 o'clock yesterday afternoon when a Spaniard named Gomez engaged in an altercation with a negress [*sic*] employed as a waitress in a restaurant…Gomez is said to have struck the woman, and she immediately appealed to her friends."

The *Hopewell Record* added, "Pandemonium ruled."

After a brief respite, the situation ignited into a full-fledged melee. "Two negroes [*sic*] were shot down by the police in an effort to dispel the rioters," the *Richmond Times-Dispatch* reported. "One is dangerously wounded, and it is understood he will not recover. The other is not dangerously injured. One member of the military police, who happened in the vicinity, also was injured by a flying bullet. His condition is not regarded as serious."

Soldiers from Camp (now Fort), Lee with militia from Hopewell and nearby Petersburg, joined with other private militia to round up any Black residents. The police station, plant jail and courtroom quickly filled. Eventually, the stations for the Norfolk and Western Railroad—the successor to the line Harris's father rode to Richmond—were turned into a guardhouse. More armed men patrolled the plant, according to a report in Dr. Lauranett Lee's book, *Making the American Dream Work: A Cultural History of African Americans in Hopewell, Virginia*.

The *Times-Dispatch* concluded, "It is estimated that several hundred shots were fired by the negroes prior to the arrival of the soldiers and militia. The latter immediately fixed bayonets and drove the angry crowd to cover. At midnight, the police authorities announced that all was quiet and that no further disturbance threatened. It is understood that arrests will follow, since the police were able to recognize a number of the ring leaders."

In a published 2001 interview, an eighty-six-year-old white woman who was five years old the night of the riot recalled the events. Evelyn Cox remembered lying on the floor with her brother and listening to violence outside her house. "Bullets were flying around, and Papa made us lie down on the floor because he was afraid a bullet might hit us. The next morning, I looked out the dining room window, and right outside was a wagon full of dead Black people…I could see their little feet hanging down—I can still see it now."

Exactly what happened remains murky. Some reports indicate that thousands were killed. Those numbers are clearly fantastic, since the riot does not appear in any historical account of major race riots in this country. Others claim that many Blacks simply left the area. That is probably unlikely, since good jobs were not common in the nearby communities, and DuPont was the only major employer in the vicinity.

The lack of information is not surprising. Despite the presence of DuPont, Hopewell was not important enough to attract much attention, although nearby Fort Lee remains an active military center. It serves as headquarters of the U.S. Army Combined Arms Support Command and hosts a couple of training schools. Harris would get to know Fort Lee well much later in his career.

Riots increased in 1919. The most dramatic took place in Chicago, when an African American teenager (Eugene Williams) drowned in Lake Michigan after violating the unofficial segregation of Chicago's beaches and being stoned by a group of white youths. His death, and the police's refusal to arrest the white man whom eyewitnesses identified as causing it, sparked a week of rioting between gangs of Black and white Chicagoans, concentrated on the South Side neighborhood surrounding the stockyards. When the riots ended on August 3, fifteen whites and twenty-three Blacks had been killed and "more than 500 people injured; an additional 1,000 black families had lost their homes when they were torched by rioters," according to History.com.

The Chicago race riot was one of twenty-five that summer, continuing a violent trend initiated the year before.

Some cities need a long time to recover from the damage to property and society. After the local turmoil, however, life in Hopewell resumed its normal chaotic way. One local minister described Hopewell as an "amazingly unreal town…a town of perilous work and perilous play…of incredible gambling halls…wild women, card sharks and con-artists." Growing rapidly, with new residents arriving daily from around the world, Hopewell became known for "its fast women and wild men. Men carried various weapons: brass knuckles, blackjacks and blades…these same men lined up around street corners for their turns in brothels," historian Edward Dent noted in his book *Race Relations in Hopewell, VA, 1635–1932*.

The good times lasted for only a short while longer. In November 1918, barely a month after the mob scene at the DuPont plant, the Great War finally ended. Without a major client, DuPont closed its Hopewell shop. However, stuck with so much land, DuPont went looking for a company to buy the vacant property. In the interim, as happened in Dendron, residents began to leave in hopes of finding employment elsewhere. A Belgium company called Tubize, which made rayon, eventually moved into the vacant site, followed by chemical plants and other firms. The economy picked up; people flowed back into the community.

As a result, when Harris and his family arrived, the city was doing well. However, the Harris family did not share in the wealth. Like many of

Hopewell's newest residents, Harris's mother was virtually unemployable. Thelma Harris could not find a job with any of the manufacturing facilities. She was relegated to the bottom level of employment, a domestic earning three dollars a week. Worse, unskilled and uneducated, Thelma found herself competing with better-educated Blacks for the few domestic positions available. In a short time, there weren't a lot of jobs anyway, as the national economy nosedived. By 1932, as the Depression deepened, an estimated half of the African American population nationwide was unemployed. Race-related violence spread. In the North, whites in some cities demanded that Blacks be fired as long as whites didn't have jobs. Lynchings grew increasingly common, jumping from six in 1932 to twenty-six nationwide a year later, according to the Tuskegee Institute Archives.

Throughout his long life, Harris felt some of the emotional hurt from those traumatic days. The family was split up. His oldest brother stayed on the farm with their grandfather, while a sister moved in with a friendly woman. The remaining children and their mother lived with the Hills, former neighbors from Surry County who had previously joined the exodus from there. They were crammed into one small house.

"It was crowded," Harris said, apparently without concern about that aspect of his life. "People always lived that way in the past."

The family moved frequently, moving from one row house to another, trying to reduce rent and costs. At age ten, Harris and his family relocated to B Village, an African American enclave that basically consisted of a series of apartment buildings built by DuPont for its workers. Also known as Davisville or the Project, B Village may have been constructed for white workers but was undergoing a transition when Harris moved there. It remains a largely Black area.

Because of the area's white background, homes in that sector did have one advantage: an indoor toilet. "I remember my sisters explaining the commode to me because I had not been used to it," Harris said.

Like many families on the margins of society, the Harrises were religious. "My mother went to the House of Prayer. Later, my three sisters went to Union Baptist Church," Harris said. Today, the church is located on Terminal Street, but Harris said that is a new location.

Harris was indifferent toward religion at first. That changed in his teens. "When I was 14, they had a tent meeting over in South B Village. They had a little church, Mt. Carmel Baptist Church. Rev. J.G.E. Horns was the pastor," Harris recalled. "The church was very small, and he wanted to have a revival." That church still exists, as well.

Revivals had been commonplace throughout the South since the 1700s but slackened during the good times of the 1920s. The Depression and resulting poverty redirected attention heavenward. Studies of fundamentalism show that revivals, typically called "gospel meetings," became an integral part of life in the 1930s. They could last three or four days, filled with singing, prayer and sermons.

"The world of Jack Benny, Lucky Strikes and Texaco, with its urban landscapes dominated by billboards, trolley cars and skyscrapers, could be induced to acknowledge God's presence and authority," writes Joel A. Carpenter in his book, *Revive Us Again: The Reawakening of American Fundamentalism.*

Such feelings were particularly poignant in the Black community. "Pining for new spiritual power and for vindication in a land that had been parched by the dry winds of modernity, fundamentalists were encouraged to expect showers of blessing. Years of ridicule and ostracism would seem worth it all when the realm of the spirit invaded the mundane world in which they lived," Carpenter notes. Biblical verses about freedom had sustained slaves for two hundred years. Those same verses now encouraged them amid overt, pervasive racism.

Harris caught that feeling while in a tent set up on a field in front of the church. "That's when I was converted," he recalled. His sisters were too busy to help with the process, so a lady across the street took him along with twenty other people to be baptized. Since no Black person was allowed to be baptized in the town, the ritual was often conducted in the river or a creek. However, with so many people in this group, the church rented a streetcar, which ran by the church anyway. They rode it to the Tabernacle Church in Petersburg. There, Fr. Gordon handled the chore, and Harris was welcomed into the religious fold. He never lost his ties to the faith and would become an ordained minister in 1959.

Initially, Harris wasn't interested in preaching. That changed over time. "I was always trying to find a way to cause people to function in a positive way," Harris explained. Eventually, public speaking became second nature to him. "If you put my hand on an altar," he said, "I'll preach you a sermon, and that's what I've been doing."

Religion for him and many in the Black community served as a kind of insulator against the surrounding hostile racial attitudes. Statistically, Blacks are more religious than their white counterparts, with more regularly attending church and believing in God. That remains true in Hopewell, where almost one-third of the nearly twenty-three thousand residents belong to evangelical Protestant churches today, according to the City Data website.

For Harris, religion provided the faith he needed to confront the racism endemic to Hopewell, a bastion of prejudice since its founding. In 1610, the colony's acting governor and chief enforcement officer, Sir Thomas Dale, issued the first laws ever published in Virginia. Called the "Lawes Divine, Morall and Martiall," they required ministers to record all christenings, marriages and deaths and were noted for their severity. He also assigned three-acre sites to early colonists, initiating the large plantations that would dominate the landscape and invite the use of slaves.

Soon after, in 1614, John Rolfe, a settler best known now for marrying the Indian princess Pocahontas, planted his first crop of hybrid tobacco using seeds from the West Indies. In three years, Virginia was exporting twenty thousand tons of tobacco, breaking the Spanish monopoly on the plant and ensuring the economic survival of the Virginia colony. However, few crops require more work. By one estimate, every laborer on a tobacco plantation tended some ten thousand plants a year, including planting, digging seedlings from the early planting bed and planting seedlings in the field. That kind of effort required willing—or unwilling—workers. The latter were not hard to find.

The Spanish had introduced slavery into the New World in the 1500s. At first, enslaved local Indians groveled for the gold the Spaniards desperately sought. However, when Indigenous people proved not hardy enough and had the annoying habit of dying rather than working, the Spanish concluded that Africans, accustomed to a hot climate, would thrive under those harsh conditions. The Portuguese supported the trade. With the assistance of African tribal leaders, happy to sell off malcontents and captured enemies, the slave business began to boom.

Virginia got its share. An extant letter written by Rolfe in January 1619 describes the arrival of a "Dutch man of war," which docked at Point-Comfort with "20…Negroes" who had been purchased in the West Indies. They are the first Black slaves recorded in the Colonies. By 1650, census figures show about four hundred Africans in the Virginia Colony, compared to about nineteen thousand white settlers.

Initially, Virginians relied on indentured servants to do the work. Those folks, having no money for tickets to the New World, paid for their passage by hiring themselves out to employers for an agreed-on number of years. By the 1660s, the labor-intensive farming outstripped the number of available indentured servants. Plantation owners began to import slaves, initially from the Caribbean, where a decline in sugar prices there encouraged owners to sell off excessive property.

Prior to that time, Blacks were not automatically enslaved. Many married and held property. For example, Anthony Johnson came to Virginia as a slave in 1621 but was freed a year later. Thirty years later, Johnson, who had taken his master's name, received 250 acres in Northampton County, becoming the first Black landowner. Reportedly, he also was the first man, Black or white, to own slaves for life. Johnson had five African slaves.

Slowly, though, Virginians tiptoed up to racism by passing laws prohibiting Blacks from owning guns in 1640, taxing Black women in 1662 and imposing life servitude for Blacks in 1667. In 1667, Virginia legislators took the final step and, by annually passing laws defining a resident's status by skin color, enshrined racism in law. After Virginia renewed the ordinance each year through 1672, similar laws were approved in 1680, 1682 and 1686.

There were still ways for a Black slave to become free. So, in 1667, Virginians closed one religion-based loophole by declaring that baptism would not free a Black slave. Two years later, legislators gave owners the right to kill a slave. The law read, "If any slave resist [sic] his master and by the extremity of the correction should chance to die, that his death not be [a] felony."

When Nathaniel Bacon, a rebellious planter, burned down Jamestown in 1676 during a vicious dispute with Governor William Berkeley of Virginia, he effectively forced planters to find slaves. Freed indentured servants had to be replaced; slaves were compelled to stay. By 1700, 13 percent of Virginia residents were slaves.

In 1705, slavery became completely encased in Virginia law with the passage of legislation declaring that "all servants imported and brought into the Country...who were not Christians in their native Country...shall be accounted and be slaves. All Negro, mulatto and Indian slaves within this dominion...shall be held to be real estate." Murder, again, was condoned. "If any slave resists his master...correcting such slave and shall happen to be killed in such correction...the master shall be free of all punishment...as if such accident never happened."

Such racial attitudes had hardened through the long years that followed. The Civil War did little to ease such tensions. By the time Harris and his family trooped into Hopewell, the racial divide was complete. The Depression just made things worse. Few escaped the turmoil of that era, but those already on the bottom economic rung, like the Harrises, suffered the most. According to a 2004 study of race relations in the 1930s, Black life was dominated by poor housing and hunger. One Southern Black resident was quoted as saying, "It's all hard, slavery and freedom, both bad when you can't eat." Homes were often decrepit, unsanitary shacks or drafty barns.

For Harris, at least, there was school. Unlike many young people, forced to drop out of school to find money in support of their families, he attended Carter G. Woodson School and graduated from there after eleventh grade. Decades later, he would win the Alumni Award from the school. Then, Woodson was located behind what is now the Hopewell main fire station. Opened in 1916, the school was set up by DuPont. "They wanted to teach Black people how to read and write so they could sign their checks," explained Dr. Ruth Jones Harris, who was married to Curtis for sixty-five years. An updated version of the school opened at its current site on Winston Churchill Drive in the 1960s and remained segregated until 1968. It became a middle school the following year.

Woodson, the namesake of the high school, was a good model for Harris. The son of former slaves and a native Virginian, Woodson became the second African American to earn a doctorate from Harvard University, just twelve years before Harris was born. Woodson, a noted author, later founded the Association for the Study of Negro Life and History and fostered Black History Month. He died in 1950, shortly before the Civil Rights Movement began.

Harris described the school as a long building with different classrooms. Unlike the students at the white school, which had steam heat, he and his classmates had "to go downstairs to the basement and bring up scuttles of coal for each class." Curtains of the wrong color hung in the auditorium. His school's colors were burgundy and green, but the curtains were hand-me-downs from all-white Hopewell High, whose colors are still blue and gold. Practically everything at the school had been previously used elsewhere. When the white school received new desks, Harris and his classmates got the old ones.

"We knew what was going on because you know how kids carve on the sides of desks and stuff. So, their names were on there." Even their paper was used. "You had to turn it over on the other side after the white kids got through with it," Harris said.

To get to school, Harris walked with his sister. Girls entered through a front door; boys went around to the back door. At Woodson, he played sports and worked for a local white bootlegger nicknamed Home Brew Daddy. "We used to go out and pick up bottles and sell them to him," Harris recalled. "I think it was a penny a bottle." He did that until Home Brew Daddy died.

By the beginning of World War II, Harris's mother gave up trying to make money as a maid—few people could afford such a luxury anymore—and turned their home into a restaurant, the Lenox Cafe. She put a big neon sign in front of the store. "We were business leaders," Harris said. His mother eventually moved to Norfolk to live with her brother, but Harris stayed in Hopewell with his sisters to run the restaurant.

"I used to have to kill all the chickens," he recalled. "When it was the weekend, you would have chicken and pigs' feet."

The clientele was all Black. The only white person they saw took care of the music machine, what Harris called a piccolo, an early jukebox. Manufacturers officially knew them as Automatic Coin-Operated Phonographs, but Southerners coined the more familiar term, which refers to an African term for a wild dance and not a musical instrument. A white repairman would visit the Harris restaurant weekly, remove the money fed into the jukebox, give some to the family and take the rest.

By then, Harris was aware of growing efforts to end racial prejudice in the country. In the 1930s, Black Virginians could have attended NAACP meetings in nearby Richmond as well as in Hampton, Norfolk and other cities. By 1934, a college chapter had opened at Virginia Union University in Richmond. Efforts to end unequal treatment began to gain support. In 1931, one Black principal started a petition drive that eventually spread across twenty-five Virginia counties and five cities and called on the state to end "racial salary differentials."

Harris might have heard about Charles Houston, a NAACP attorney who led a group of investigators to film school conditions around the state, documenting the underfunded status of Black schools. Houston spoke to students at Virginia Union in 1935. Involved in civil rights cases from 1930 through his death in 1950, Houston graduated from Harvard Law School in 1922 and was the first African American editor of the *Harvard Law Review*. He developed the strategy that led to the end of "separate but equal" laws. Called "The Man Who Killed Jim Crow," Houston stressed the inequality of the "separate but equal" doctrine in education.

Motivated by the racism he experienced during two years in the U.S. Army, Houston said, "The hate and scorn showered on us Negro officers by our fellow Americans convinced me that there was no sense in my dying for a world ruled by them. I made up my mind that, if I got through this war, I would study law and use my time fighting for men who could not strike back.…This fight for equality of educational opportunity [was] not an isolated struggle. All our struggles must tie in together and support one another.…We must remain on the alert and push the struggle farther with all our might."

Harris certainly knew about C.A. Robbins, a local doctor who was active in the NAACP. Eventually, Robbins and other activists would choose Harris to take over the NAACP office in Hopewell. He was in his early twenties then, one of the few young people in Hopewell. Most had left to join the military or for better jobs. Harris, however, would devote most of his succeeding years to Hopewell, gradually becoming a national figure as he fought against the smothering racial attitudes that surrounded him.

CHAPTER 2

RACIAL ENVIRONMENT

LEGAL CASES, *PLESSY V. FERGUSON*

By the time Harris was born, the inferior status of Blacks in both Virginia and the rest of the country was thoroughly wrapped in legal tape. No state did more than Virginia to make sure anyone with scissors was not given a chance to cut any of it.

The early laws passed in the antebellum seventeenth, eighteenth and nineteenth centuries were no longer in force, washed away in the blood of the Civil War. The Thirteenth, Fourteenth and Fifteenth Amendments to the Constitution were now the legal guidelines and were supposed to end any prejudicial treatment.

Passed in 1864, while the war still raged, the Thirteenth Amendment banned slavery and involuntary servitude except for duly convicted criminals. It was the natural follow-up to President Abraham Lincoln's Emancipation Proclamation, which, as of January 1, 1963, freed slaves in the rebellious states.

The Fourteenth Amendment continued the process of giving Black Americans full citizenship rights by providing a definition of citizenship so broad that it encompassed everyone in the United States. Approved in 1868, three years after the war ended, its main purpose was to counter the 1857 Supreme Court's Dred Scott decision, which declared a slave could not obtain freedom simply by entering a state that banned slavery. In essence, the court had declared Blacks were not citizens of the United States. Eleven years later, they were reinstated.

The Fourteenth Amendment also banned state and local governments from unfairly stripping residents of "life, liberty, or property" and was designed to ensure that the Bill of Rights provisions already in the Constitution were extended to the former slaves. Finally, the amendment guaranteed equal protection under the law and would later underpin a 1954 Supreme Court decision that finally ended the separate but equal education systems in this country.

The Fifteenth Amendment directly prohibited anyone being denied the right to vote "on account of race, color, or previous condition of servitude." Virginia and two other states, Mississippi and Georgia, were specifically required to ratify this amendment to regain their status in the Union. The amendment did not receive unanimous congressional approval. Some thirteen members of Congress abstained, unhappy the new law did not restrict states from limiting voting through poll taxes and other means. They must have been clairvoyant. On the other hand, they only had to look at existing state laws to see what was going to happen.

States had already started the process of ensuring Blacks—free or enslaved—remained second-class citizens even before the Civil War. Many later rulings were based on an 1849 Massachusetts decision. That state's supreme court then held that the general school committee of Boston could create separate schools for Black and white children. Chief Justice Lemuel Shaw of the Massachusetts Supreme Court wrote that, while all people are equal under the law, "when this great principle comes to be applied to the actual and various conditions of persons in society, it will not warrant the assertion that men and women are legally clothed with the same civil and political powers." Based on that logic, he said that Boston could create separate schools for children of different ages, sexes and colors.

Shaw's opinion carried great weight. He served as chief justice of the Massachusetts Supreme Judicial Court for thirty years and wrote an estimated 2,200 decisions. "At the time of his appointment to the bench, American law was still in its formative period. No other state judge through his opinions alone had so great an influence on the course of American law," wrote historian Leonard W. Levy. In 1881, in *The Common Law*, Oliver Wendell Holmes Jr. said of Shaw that "few have lived who were his equals in their understanding of the grounds of public policy to which all laws must ultimately be referred. It is this that made him…the greatest magistrate which this country has produced."

Shaw, father-in-law of *Moby-Dick* author Herman Melville, is better known today for developing the "reasonable doubt" concept in law, but this 1849 ruling had more impact. Other states did not hesitate to follow Shaw's guidance, including Ohio and Indiana. In the Hoosier State, for example, laws banning intermarriage were upheld as legal in 1871, deemed under the police power of the state.

The 1869 Slaughterhouse Cases in Louisiana involved similar issues. The dispute grew out of a seemingly unrelated decision by the Louisiana state legislature to award a monopoly to one slaughterhouse. Competitors filed suit, arguing that the legislation violated the Fourteenth Amendment by depriving them of property without due process. In 1973, the U.S. Supreme Court then upheld the monopoly in the first legal test of the amendment. The Justices ruled 5–4 that the Fourteenth Amendment was designed to protect emancipated slaves and that federal protection of civil rights did not interfere with a state's jurisdiction over its residents or the property rights of businesses. The decision reduced the power of the federal government while undercutting protection for former slaves.

The various state laws soon picked up national endorsements. Congress got the ball rolling in 1894 by repealing forty-two of the forty-nine sections of the civil rights enforcement provisions approved during Reconstruction. Two years later, the Supreme Court chimed in, basing its decision on Judge Shaw's ruling fifty years earlier. In its ruling, the United States's highest court voted 7–1 (one justice did not participate) to legalize segregation.

The case was spurred by an 1890 state law called the Louisiana Separate Car Act. The new ordinance stated that all railway companies carrying passengers in Louisiana "shall provide equal but separate accommodations for the white and colored races, by providing two or more passenger coaches for each passenger train, or by dividing the passenger coaches by a partition so as to secure separate accommodations." That's the first reference to what became known as the "separate but equal" doctrine that was so much a part of Black lives from the 1870s through the 1950s.

Passed by the state legislature in a 23–6 vote, the law drew wide support from the white population, but there was some opposition. Republican legislator Henry Demas said the bill came from the "ranks of Democratic Senators who pandered to the needs of the lower classes" and reflected the ideas of people with no "social or moral standing in the community."

The *Daily Picayune*, the state's largest and most influential newspaper, however, insisted there was "almost unanimous demand on the part of white people of the State for the enactment of the law," which would "increase the comfort for the traveling public." The New Orleans–based newspaper added—accurately—that the law would align Louisiana with southern states.

The law continued, "No person or persons shall be permitted to occupy seats in coaches, other than the ones assigned to them, on account of the race they belong to." Someone violating the law "shall be liable to a fine of twenty-five dollars, or in lieu thereof to imprisonment for a period of not more than twenty days in the parish prison." That was also true for any officer of any railroad who deliberately disobeyed the law. The legislators thoughtfully added that anyone who refused to comply could be barred from riding a train and that "the railway company shall [not] be liable for damages in any of the courts of this state." Nannies were exempt: "Nothing in this act shall be construed as applying to nurses attending children of the other race."

The law, created in a pre-automobile period when railroads carried the bulk of long-distance passengers, naturally generated a stir. A group of Black professionals in New Orleans decided to test the legislation by convincing a Creole resident to sit in the white section of an interstate train. The Citizens' Committee to Test the Constitutionality of the Separate Car Law (Comité des Citoyens) chose a Creole named Daniel Desdunes, who looked white. He was an easy choice: his father was a founding member of the committee. Desdunes would later move to Omaha, Nebraska and, among other activities, head the band at Fr. Flanagan's famous Boys Town there.

Before Desdunes went to trial, however, Louisiana district court judge John Ferguson, a Massachusetts native who had moved to New Orleans, declared in a separate case that the new state law could not be applied to interstate travelers.

With one success under its belt, the committee decided to next test the law with a passenger riding from one town to another inside Louisiana and hired attorney Albion W. Tourgée, a white, Ohio-born former superior court judge who was then living in New York. Tourgée had a lengthy history in civil rights. In 1866, then twenty-eight and a resident of North Carolina, he published two newspapers while participating in various groups focused on racial equality. Two years later, he was elected a state superior court judge in North Carolina. His decision created a furor. Called a carpetbagger, he was labeled "the most thoroughly hated man in North Carolina."

In time, Tourgée gained national attention with an autobiography and then a novel. However, his syndicated newspaper columns denouncing segregation were what drew the committee's interest. Then in his sixties, he readily took on the challenge as the lead attorney.

Homer Plessy agreed to be the defendant for purposes of the second test case. Plessy was a shoemaker from New Orleans, and he and his family easily passed for white, just like Desdunes before him. After all, Plessy only had one Black relative, a great-grandmother. Photos of him show a light-skinned man with a full beard. Under state law, however, he was considered Black, an "octoroon." Ironically, as a child born after the Civil War, Plessy initially attended integrated schools and faced no restrictions on travel or marriage. That changed in 1877 when federal troops were withdrawn to mark the "end" of Reconstruction. Louisiana quickly changed its laws to parallel similar cross-racial restrictions in other states.

On Tuesday, June 7, 1892, Plessy purchased a first-class ticket for a trip from New Orleans to Covington, Louisiana, on the East Louisiana Railroad at a station at the corner of Press Street and Royal—today not far from the home of the Louisiana Supreme Court. There is also a marker on the site commemorating Plessy's case. Plessy sat down nonchalantly in the whites-only car, which was cleaner and nicer than the Black car. When a conductor—primed by the committee—came in and requested Plessy relocate to the black-only car, Plessy declined. Being seven-eighths white exempted him, he said. The conductor rejected that logic and, as agreed, had Plessy arrested. A private detective, also hired by the committee, was on hand, too. After an overnight stay in the jail, Plessy was freed on bond. He faced twenty days in jail or a twenty-five-dollar fine if convicted.

The case went to Louisiana district court, where Judge Ferguson, this time, upheld the law. He ruled the state "had the constitutional power to regulate railroad companies operating solely within its borders." His decision was appealed to the state supreme court, which upheld the lower court ruling. The Louisiana high court backed the legislature and noted the racial element in the decision: "The object of the [Fifteenth] Amendment was undoubtedly to enforce the absolute equality of the two races before the law, but, in the nature of things, it could not have been intended to abolish distinctions based upon color, or to enforce social, as distinguished from political, equality, or a commingling of the two races upon terms unsatisfactory to either."

From there, the case finally made its way onto the Supreme Court docket in 1896. Tourgée relied on the Thirteenth and Fourteenth Amendments for his argument, saying that the law perpetuated the "essential features of slavery." The Supreme Court overwhelmingly disagreed.

Judge Henry Billings Brown, a Massachusetts native who usually took a centrist position, wrote the majority opinion. Then living in Michigan, Brown was described as "a privileged son of the Yankee merchant class…a reflexive social elitist whose opinions of women, African-Americans, Jews, and immigrants now seem odious, even if they were unexceptional for their time" in a commentary written after his death, according to his biographer Francis A. Helminski. Brown insisted that the only issue in the case was whether or not the statute was reasonable. The court, he continued, was "at liberty to act with reference to the established usages, customs, and traditions of the people, and with a view to the promotion of their comfort, and the preservation of the public peace and good order."

In his opinion, Brown said that Tourgée's claims contained an "underlying fallacy…in the assumption that the enforced separation of the two races stamps the colored race with a badge of inferiority. If this be so, it is not by reason of anything found in the act, but solely because the colored race chooses to put that construction upon it."

The logic, which today seems stunningly naive, nevertheless separated political from social claims of equality. Blacks and whites were equal politically and protected by the three amendments, but no law could eliminate racist attitudes or overshadow obvious physical differences. After all, Brown said, the simple fact that Blacks must sit someplace away from white passengers did not imply superiority or inferiority.

The lone dissenting judge, John Marshall Harlan, disagreed vehemently. Relying on information supplied by the committee that brought the lawsuit, he wrote, "The state [is regulating] the use of a public highway by citizens of the United States solely upon the basis of race." A native of Kentucky who openly socialized with Blacks and Indians, Harlan was the oldest serving member of that court. He pointed out that the law "had its origin in the purpose, not so much to exclude white persons from railroad cars occupied by blacks, as to exclude colored people from coaches occupied by or assigned to white persons."

He added:

> Our Constitution is color-blind, and neither knows nor tolerates classes among citizens. In respect of civil rights, all citizens are equal before the law.…In my opinion, the judgment this day rendered will, in time, prove to be quite as pernicious as the decision made by this tribunal in the Dred Scott case.…The present decision, it may well be apprehended, will not only stimulate aggressions, more or less brutal and irritating, upon the admitted rights of colored citizens, but will encourage the belief that it is possible, by means of state enactments, to defeat the beneficent purposes which the people of the United States had in view when they adopted the recent amendments of the Constitution.

He was correct. The decision turned segregation into a southern institution, as pervasive and insidious as slavery, by galvanizing state legislatures to pass laws enshrining the "separate but equal" doctrine. After a brief stay in jail, Plessy would become an insurance agent; he died in 1925. His name, and the ruling his efforts helped spawn, would live on into the 1950s.

Virginia did not sit idly by amid the flurry of legal decisions. For the commonwealth, *Plessy v. Ferguson* was only the latest legal effort to ensure white control of the legislature and second-class status for Black residents.

The end of the Civil War and Virginia's subsequent defeat had led legislators to attempt to create laws supporting the Thirteenth, Fourteenth and Fifteenth Amendments. In its effort to return to the Union, the state held a constitutional convention in 1869. Then, under the direction of John Underwood, Virginia Republicans—whose national party had been founded in 1854 principally to end slavery—drafted a document granting full suffrage for all males twenty-one years or older, including African Americans. The effort worked: the new law also helped return Virginia to good standing in the United States.

A New Yorker, Underwood had moved to a family farm in Virginia and once been forced to flee angry neighbors outraged by his abolitionist views. He advocated for full suffrage for Blacks and for women of any color. Appointed a federal judge in Virginia by President Lincoln, Underwood used his position to seize the estates of Confederates in order to apply what he called "retributive justice." Ironically, his wife was a cousin of General Thomas "Stonewall" Jackson.

Within a few years, however, Underwood's enlightened approach alienated the conservative wing of the Democratic Party and racist Republicans. In 1876, the Virginia legislature required a poll tax, hoping that poor Blacks could be excluded, but that lasted only six years before reformers, called Readjusters, eliminated it. That brief light of enlightened policies in Virginia was quickly doused. Outraged, Democrats wrested back control of the state legislature and passed the Anderson-McCormick Act in 1884. The new law allowed the general assembly, under Democratic control, to name all members of electoral boards in all counties and cities. The boards then appointed local voter registrars, who kept segregated lists of voters. In case of appeal, the electoral boards named the judges to hear the cases. The resulting corruption created an uproar as Democrats stuffed ballots in districts that were predominately Black and/or Republican. Bribes flowed, guaranteeing Democrats stayed in control of state politics.

In response, under enormous pressure from state residents infuriated by the corruption, the Virginia legislature passed the Walton Act in 1894. This law, named for Morgan Walton, who represented Page and Shenandoah

Counties, essentially disenfranchised voters based on literacy. It stipulated that ballots must be uniform and issued by the state, not by political parties; contain no symbols or party designations; and require a degree of literacy to mark properly. Voters had to draw a line through unacceptable candidates, leaving only the chosen candidate's name untouched.

Not surprisingly, more than 50 percent of Virginia's African Americans— and a good chunk of whites—were illiterate. If a voter who could not read managed to get a ballot, he could ask for help from a designated constable, but there was no guarantee the constable would provide the correct information.

One historian noted that the act sliced into the Republican Party's black base. "[T]he estimated percentage of Negroes who cast their ballots for the opposition fell from 46 percent in 1893 to 2 percent in 1897...The Walton Law ended most actual voting," wrote Morgan J. Kousser, California Institute of Technology history and social sciences professor.

The Populist Movement that arose in the 1890s, however, undercut some of these efforts as Democratic Party factions used the same illegal methods to steal elections from each other. The resulting accusations and acrimony led to the state convention to create a new constitution.

The Encyclopedia Virginia notes that the delegates did take positive steps to help the state. They developed a process to regulate the railroads, created workmen's compensation, set up a commission to work on industrialization and provided some economic stability within Virginia. However, the encyclopedia notes, the main focus of the session "of the convention movement was to deprive African-Americans of the suffrage and thereby eliminate the Democrats' need to cheat in order to win."

To make sure that white control could not be undermined, state officials called for a new constitutional convention. Just twenty-two years before Harris was born, the Virginia Constitutional Convention rewrote the Virginia constitution to maintain white supremacy. Produced during what later became known as the Progressive era, a thirty-year stretch marked by the end of monopolies and the passage of laws to protect workers and improve food production, among other important reforms, white Virginians reverted to racist concepts, making sure they disenfranchised their Black counterparts.

Between 1901 and 1902, eighty-eight Democrats, eleven Republicans and one Independent met in Richmond for two sessions to determine the necessary changes. Conservative Democrats had boycotted the 1869 session that equalized treatment of Blacks; now, they turned out in force. One of the delegates vigorously rejected the majority's efforts. Republican delegate

Albert P. Gillespie charged that "the Negro vote of this Commonwealth must be destroyed to prevent Democratic officers from stealing their votes, for it seems that, as long as there is a Negro vote to be stolen, there will be a Democratic election officer ready to steal it."

Convention president John Goode ignored such insults and stated, "The right of suffrage is not a natural right. It is a social right and must necessarily be regulated by society. Virginia, within her borders, can regulate it according to her own sovereign will and pleasure, provided she does not violate the Constitution of the United States." He particularly opposed the Fifteenth Amendment, which guaranteed Negro suffrage, calling it not only "a stupendous blunder, but a crime against civilization and Christianity" that had been ratified by southern states only "under the rule of bayonet."

The biggest argument centered on concerns that any new laws could disenfranchise poor, illiterate whites right along with Blacks. Delegate W. Gordon Robertson pointed out that "the best thing that we can do to get around the Fifteenth Amendment is to appoint men in every county who will use favoritism towards the white man as against the black man. There are thousands upon thousands of white men in our mountains who can neither read nor understand this Constitution, whom these gentlemen are willing to have vote, and who would not be eligible to vote under the provisions of this Constitution, if this temporary understanding clause is properly administered."

Finally, led by publisher Carter Glass, who later would be involved in the creation of the Federal Reserve System, the delegates approved a prepaid poll tax that was up to date for three years. A voter had to submit a written application for registration. All Civil War veterans, North and South, and their sons were exempted from any of these onerous requirements. Tax collectors did not attempt to collect the poll tax. Instead, voters were expected to pay it and then know how to register to vote. That required visits to different commissioners, who developed the habit of leaving their offices when Republicans or Black voters came by or of asking meaningless questions until the would-be voter gave up.

Both parties found a way to make money on the deal by charging public officials a portion of their salaries to pay poll taxes for men (and, later, women) with reliable voting records. The new restrictions were supposed to be temporary, ending in 1904. Actually, they endured into the 1970s.

The delegates decided voters were not likely to disenfranchise themselves, so did not present the new constitution for ratification. The Virginia Supreme Court later turned aside challenges to its validity.

The delegates had done their job well. The Encyclopedia Virginia recorded that "in the 1900 presidential election, 264,240 Virginia men voted; in 1904, a mere 135,865 did, a reduction in the whole number of votes of 48.6 percent. The Republican vote fell from 43.8 percent to 35.2 percent of the total. The number of white voters declined by about 50 percent, and the number of black votes declined by about 90 percent and remained insignificantly small in all but a few communities until the mid-1960s."

Glass, later a U.S. representative and a senator, led much of the debate and wrote glowingly about the results of the convention, although actually, more whites than Blacks were disenfranchised. In fact, for years after the 1902 constitution went into effect, adults in Virginia consistently voted in the smallest proportion compared with other states.

As a result, until Harris was in his sixties, he had little say in the political life of his state. One more law, passed the year he was born, made sure voting wasn't the only thing he and other African Americans could be deprived of in the Commonwealth of Virginia.

CHAPTER 3

SOCIAL UNREST

LYNCHING, DESEGREGATION EFFORTS, EUGENICS

D uring the first fifty years of Rev. Curtis Harris's life, he was considered almost a nonperson in Virginia. He could be killed almost with impunity. Lynching, after all, was named for Virginian Charles Lynch, who presided over illegal trials of Tories after the Revolutionary War. In his day, those convicted in his "court" faced loss of property, whipping or similar punishments. In time, however, the term *lynching* was reserved for death.

In 1928, Virginia became the first state to define lynching as a state crime, but no white person in the state was ever convicted of lynching a Black person, although, between 1880 and 1930, at least seventy Blacks died that way. Instead, the law was used to convict whites who attacked other whites, not whites who strung up a Black victim.

Ironically, Virginians were, surprisingly, safer from lynching than those in other southern states because, researchers found, community leaders preferred law and order to mob rule. That doesn't mean there weren't lynchings. According to Tuskegee Institute archival records, between 1882 and 1968, 100 Virginians were lynched—83 percent of whom were Black. That compares to 493 in Texas, 251 in Tennessee and 581 in Mississippi, the highest number recorded. On average, between 1889 to 1923, the year before Harris was born, southern states annually recorded 50 to 100 lynchings.

Harris also could have been killed through legal methods under the guise of a pseudoscience called eugenics, which was designed to "improve" humans by eliminating hereditary ailments or flaws that could creep into the genes. The idea was first suggested by the famed Greek philosopher Plato, some 2,300 years ago, in his Socratic dialogue known as *The Republic*. He thought wise members of society could select people capable of reproducing.

The Romans followed eugenic ideas, as well. According to the Roman philosopher Seneca, "We put down mad dogs; we kill the wild, untamed ox; we use the knife on sick sheep to stop their infecting the flock; we destroy abnormal offspring at birth; children, too, if they are born weak or deformed, we drown. Yet this is not the work of anger, but of reason—to separate the sound from the worthless."

Modern eugenics, however, was the mid-nineteenth-century brainchild of Sir Francis Galton, a cousin of Charles Darwin, whose research into evolution introduced the concept of natural selection to a stunned world. Galton focused his attention on the issue, applying statistics to the study of human differences and intelligence. He coined the term *eugenics* and was the first to study the connection between intelligence and success. In 1863, he proposed that talented people would produce better offspring if they married other talented people. In his book *Hereditary Genius*, Galton wrote:

I propose to show in this book that a man's natural abilities are derived by inheritance, under exactly the same limitations as are the form and physical features of the whole organic world. Consequently, as it is easy, notwithstanding those limitations, to obtain by careful selection a permanent breed of dogs or horses gifted with peculiar powers of running, or of doing anything else, so it would be quite practicable to produce a highly gifted race of men by judicious marriages during several consecutive generations.

That view was later tied to the studies of Austrian monk Gregor Mendel, whose painstaking studies of peas showed how parental characteristics were inherited by their offspring. Scientists studying the research in the first years of the twentieth century concluded incorrectly that, as Galton suggested, the same concepts worked for humans. Everyone was eager to improve the social and intellectual character of man. Race could not be isolated from that effort.

Stanford University president David Starr Jordan tied the ideas together by equating "race and blood" in a 1902 speech. Human qualities and conditions, like talent and poverty, were passed through the blood, he insisted.

The Nazis borrowed the concept and were positive that Jews, disabled people, homosexuals and others fell into the "bad" category. In the United States, Blacks and immigrants were labeled defective. The pseudoscience was not discredited until after World War II with advances in genetic research and better understanding of DNA. Until then, though, political leaders promoted eugenics. Naturally, Virginia was in the forefront in that area, too.

In 1691, Virginia became the first colony to outlaw interracial marriage. Maryland followed its lead a year later. Many other states joined in. By 1913, more than half of the then forty-eight states had the same law on their books. Six states thoughtfully put that provision in their constitutions. By the start of World War II, thirty American states had passed eugenic laws, led by California.

For the idea to work, officials needed to define racial identities. As a result, in 1705, Virginia's leaders began labeling. "Mulatto," for example, became the tag for anyone who was "the child of an Indian and the child, grandchild, or great grandchild, of a negro [sic]." Some eighty years later, state officials went a step further and applied the mulatto identification to "every person who shall have one-fourth part or more of negro [sic] blood."

The name for anyone with 25 percent "negro blood" was changed to "colored person" after the Civil War. The percentage was dropped to one-sixteenth in 1910. Everyone else was white.

As eugenics became accepted, various institutions stepped up to help weed out those who, they believed, would undermine the human race. In 1904, the Carnegie Institution built a laboratory at Cold Spring Harbor, New York, where names of Americans were collected on millions of index cards in an effort to determine which bloodlines should be eliminated. The Rockefeller Foundation worked overseas to fund German eugenics programs, including one that employed and trained Dr. Joseph Mengele, who later used his knowledge on hapless inmates at the Auschwitz concentration camp.

Mengele's murderous approach was based on suggestions made by American scholars that were included in a 1911 study funded by the Carnegie Foundation and titled *Preliminary Report of the Committee of the Eugenic Section of the American Breeder's Association to Study and to Report on the Best Practical Means for Cutting Off the Defective Germ-Plasm in the Human Population*. Among the optimum solutions suggested by this report with its ungainly title was the legalization of euthanasia, using gas chambers.

That idea was fostered by Paul Popenoe, then a U.S. Army venereal disease specialist and later the father of marriage counseling. He cowrote a textbook titled *Applied Eugenics*, which explained, "From an historical point of view, the first method which presents itself is execution.…Its value in keeping up the standard of the race should not be underestimated." In one chapter, the book called for "Lethal Selection," which advocated for "the destruction of the individual by some adverse feature of the environment, such as excessive cold, or bacteria, or by bodily deficiency."

While many eugenics practitioners sincerely thought they were improving society by benignly not caring for disabled newborns or directly applying lethal methods to adults, the main thrust of the eugenics effort was in the realm of segregation and racial policies. Virginia eagerly embraced that approach, finding a solution to racial concerns in a scalpel.

The issue had first been discussed openly via an 1893 letter in the *Virginia Medical Monthly*. Dr. Hunter Holmes McGuire, a Richmond doctor and then president of the American Medical Association, wrote to ask if there were "some scientific explanation of the sexual perversion in the Negro of the present day." Dr. G. Frank Lydston, a Chicago physician, replied that African American men raped white women because of "hereditary influences descending from the uncivilized ancestors of our Negroes." Lydston suggested as a solution to perform surgical castration, which "prevents the criminal from perpetuating his kind."

The next step was to create the legal framework to prevent pregnancies. In 1924, the same year Harris was born, legislators approved a series of race-based laws. The best known was the Racial Integrity Act (RIA), which set in place regulations against racial mixing and allowed sterilization of women considered unfit. To the white political leaders, that was any Black woman.

The root source of the bill was racism, something well recognized by proponents. "The true motive was the maintenance of white supremacy and black economic and social inferiority—racism, pure and simple.... Eugenical ideology...provided intellectual fuel to the racist fires," wrote Paul Lombardo, a legal scholar who teaches at the University of Virginia and has written extensively on the legal case that eventually upheld the law.

Supporters did not deny that. Lothrop Stoddard, a Massachusetts-born lawyer, told the legislature that "white race-purity is the cornerstone of our civilization. Its mongrelization with non-white blood, particularly with Negro blood, would spell the downfall of our civilization." Stoddard divided the white race into three units: Nordic (the best), Alpine and Mediterranean. He thought "the colored race" was "naturally inferior."

Stoddard's ideas would eventually dominate American thinking. For example, also in 1924, the United States approved the Immigration Act, which included strict quotas to limit immigrants from countries that eugenicists like Stoddard thought contained "inferior" stock.

President Calvin Coolidge signed the bill into law. He was a supporter. Previously, when serving as Warren G. Harding's vice president, he said,

"America should be kept American....Biological laws show that Nordics deteriorate when mixed with other races."

Virginia had plenty of other precedents to draw upon. The RIA also relied on aspects of the South African apartheid system to make sure Blacks were completely identified and restricted. The law mandated racial registration certificates and strictly defined who could be considered white. All of that was based on pseudoscience and the "dangers" posed by mixed-race marriages.

Some of those views filtered into American theater via 1927's *Showboat*, considered the first modern Broadway musical. In it, biracial singer Julie LaVerne is arrested for having married a white man. Producer Flo Ziegfeld even hesitated to put the show on because of its racial content. However, lyricist Oscar Hammerstein II and composer Jerome Kern insisted the story be unchanged in protest of the legislation.

According to the law:

> *It shall hereafter be unlawful for any white person in this State to marry any save a white person, or a person with no other admixture of blood than white and American Indian....The term "white person" shall apply only to such person as has no trace whatever of any blood other than Caucasian; but persons who have one-sixteenth or less of the blood of the American Indian and have no other non-Caucasic blood shall be deemed to be white persons.*

Alabama and Georgia eventually added the Virginia statute to their books.

Virginia increased its eugenic caseload with a 1926 case involving a young white woman, Carrie Buck, who was identified as a "genetic threat to society." The state insisted she was immoral. Actually, Carrie Buck had been raped, and family members committed her to shield the family's reputation. The resulting suit, titled *Buck v. Bell*, legitimized sterilization nationwide.

The Supreme Court added its weight to the case, with Judge Oliver Wendell Holmes Jr. leading the support by saying famously that "three generations of imbeciles were enough." He wrote, "It is better for all the world, if instead of waiting to execute degenerate offspring for crime, or to let them starve for their imbecility, society can prevent those who are manifestly unfit from continuing their kind."

Years later, Nazi leaders on trial in Nuremburg quoted Holmes's words in their defense. Hitler also cited such American eugenic theories in his book *Mein Kampf*. His approach won wide support in this country. Nazi propaganda was republished in English, and Nazi scientific exhibits went on display, including one at the annual meeting of the American Public Health Association in 1934.

Virginia did not repeal its sterilization laws until 1979, long after other states did so. In many instances, a sheriff would drive into mountain villages and simply take people to institutions where they were forcibly sterilized, unaware of what the operation was for. Overall, the state eventually sterilized more than 7,325 people, continuing the practice almost alone after other states ceased. About half of the victims were called "mentally ill"; the rest were "mentally deficient." More than 60 percent were female. At least 22 percent were considered Black, although the percentage was probably higher because of the way the state classified its residents.

Virginia state officials also made sure the right people were operated on by creating a Bureau of Vital Statistics in 1912 to keep careful tabs on racial identities and made sure everyone knew exactly which group they belonged to.

For many years, the bureau was led by Dr. Walter Plecker, a small-town doctor whose dictates stereotyped all residents. Known for not smiling, the Virginian supported Nazi efforts to "cleanse" Germany's population. In 1935, Plecker sent a letter to Walter Gross, the director of Germany's Bureau of Human Betterment and Eugenics. In it, Plecker explained Virginia's racial purity laws and requested his name be added to a mailing list for bulletins from Gross's department. Plecker also praised the German government for sterilizing six hundred Algerian children born to German women and Black fathers. "I hope this work is complete and not one has been missed," he wrote. "I sometimes regret that we have not the authority to put some measures in practice in Virginia."

Plecker was also a cofounder of the Anglo-Saxon Clubs of America (ASCOA), which was created in Richmond in 1922. Committed to racial purity, the ASCOA was headed by renowned pianist John Powell, ethnologist Earnest Sevier Cox and Plecker. Cox, who died in 1966, produced a book titled *White America*, which used eugenics to support his racist theories. A Tennessee native, he was convinced American civilization would collapse if races mixed. As a result, in the 1920s, he worked with Dr. Marcus Garvey to promote the Pan-Americanism Movement, which encouraged the return of African Americans to their native land. Powell, another Virginian, used his fame to promote racism.

To Plecker, anyone with a hint of African American heritage was Black, including Indians. He undermined Native culture by claiming that Indians were "mixed-blooded negroes [*sic*]." He had Indians reclassified as "colored" and destroyed their ability to obtain state and/or federal status based on their Indian heritage. A member of a conservative Presbyterian sect that believed the Bible was infallible and condoned segregation, Plecker accepted the church philosophy that God flooded the earth and destroyed Sodom to express his anger at racial interbreeding. "Let us turn a deaf ear to those who would interpret Christian brotherhood as racial equality," Plecker wrote in a 1925 essay.

As head of the Bureau of Vital Statistics, Plecker held the power to issue birth, death and marriage certificates. With a single notation, he could assign "negro" status to anyone, ending their hope of legal or social status. His approach was extremely heavy-handed. For instance, he forced school superintendents to exclude mixed-race children from white schools. He also ordered dead people of "questionable ancestry" exhumed from white cemeteries to be reinterred elsewhere.

Plecker's letters to applicants were caustic and blunt.

> Dear Madam,
> We have report of the birth of your child, July 30th, 1923, signed by _____, midwife. She says that you are white and that the father of the child is white.
> We have a correction to this certificate sent to us from the City Health Department at Lynchburg in which they say that the father of this child is a negro.
> This is to give you warning that this is a mulatto child and you cannot pass it off as white. A new law passed by the last Legislature says that if a child has one drop of negro blood in it, it cannot be counted as white.
> You will have to do something about this matter and see that this child is not allowed to mix with white children. It cannot go to white schools and can never marry a white person in Virginia.
> It is an awful thing.

Another letter to a midwife:

> Dear Madam,
> This is to notify you that it is a penitentiary offense to willfully state that a child is white when it is colored. You have made yourself liable to very serious trouble by doing this thing. What have you got to say about it?

Plecker relied on birth certificates, marriage licenses, tax records and gossip to determine racial identity. He even "corrected" birth certificates if he thought a person was trying to "pass" as white.

The efforts of Plecker's agency were unsurpassed, leading to this boast in a 1943 letter: "Our own indexed birth and marriage records, showing race, reach back to 1853. Such a study has probably never been made before.... Hitler's genealogical study of the Jews is not more complete." Dr. Plecker stayed at his post until 1946, guaranteeing strict enforcement of the laws.

When some legislators opposed including Indians in the list of Blacks, the Virginia General Assembly passed another racial integrity law in 1930. Under this statute, people with one-quarter Indian blood and less than one-sixteenth Black blood were classified as Indians—they had to live on a reservation, segregated from whites.

Other Virginia leaders objected to what was being done on behalf of eugenics. They thought the pace was too slow. For example, Dr. Joseph DeJarnette, director of the Western State Hospital, located in Staunton, Virginia, wrote:

> *Germany in six years has sterilized about 80,000 of her unfit while the United States—with approximately twice the population—has only sterilized about 27,869 in the past 20 years....The fact that there are 12,000,000 defectives in the U.S. should arouse our best endeavors to push this procedure to the maximum....The Germans are beating us at our own game.*

One of the leaders of the eugenics movement was the University of Virginia School of Medicine. A student enrolled there noted in a published 1934 article: "In Germany, Hitler has decreed that about 400,000 persons be sterilized. This is a great step in eliminating the racial deficients [*sic*]."

Only after World War II, when the world realized how far the Nazis had carried their genetic program, did the full impact of eugenics become evident.

Harris would have had difficulty learning about eugenics or even the role Virginia played in its development. That's because, like all Black Virginians, his skin color also reduced his educational opportunities and career choices to a very narrow roster. For example, the University of Virginia (UVA), founded by Thomas Jefferson and a center of the state's intellectual life, did not allow a Black student to enroll until 1950.

That didn't mean Black residents didn't try to get into the University of Virginia, one of the state's most prestigious schools. In 1935, for example, as part of a coordinated effort orchestrated by the National Association for the Advancement of Colored People (NAACP), Richmond native Alice Jackson, a graduate of Virginia Union, applied there, but was rejected.

The official announcement that accompanied her rejection said:

The education of white and colored persons in the same schools is contrary to the long established and fixed policy of the Commonwealth of Virginia. Therefore, for this and other good and sufficient reasons not necessary to be herein enumerated, the rector and board of visitors of the University of Virginia direct the dean of the department of graduate studies to refuse respectfully the pending application of a colored student.

Outraged Black organizations threatened to sue. That forced the state to pass the Dovell Act, which created a fund for Jackson and other Black Virginians to attend out-of-state schools when no in-state equivalent was available. Jackson went to Columbia University in New York City for her master's degree. After graduation, she couldn't find a teaching position in Virginia. She taught in Florida for forty-five years and was finally recognized for her pioneering efforts by a resolution passed by the Virginia assembly in 1990. She died in 2001.

At first, Blacks were able to apply to state universities for graduate programs because Virginia State College, the state's only public university for African Americans, didn't have any professors with doctorate degrees until 1937 and couldn't offer graduate programs until then. But the fact that Blacks could fill out application forms didn't mean they would be accepted.

About fifteen years after Jackson headed north, a Howard University graduate named Gregory Swanson, who was interested in studying law at UVA, filed his application. Swanson was originally rejected because of his skin color, too.

The board of visitors wrote:

The applicant is a colored man. The Constitution and the laws of the State of Virginia provide that white and colored shall not be taught in the same schools. It has been the traditional policy of the University of Virginia to provide for the difference between tuition costs at the University of Virginia and the cost at other comparable institutions for colored applicants who may not be admitted to the University of Virginia Law School by reason of the law of this State. The Board of Visitors feels that it is obligated to comply with the Constitution and laws of the State of Virginia. Therefore, the application has been denied.

To gain admission to the state's only state-supported law school, Swanson fought a lengthy court battle with the help of the NAACP and future Supreme Court justice Thurgood Marshall. Eventually, he was allowed into the university. Not everyone in the student body approved. When Swanson went to the opening football game that fall, students waved Confederate flags, and the school band played "Dixie." While publicly speaking out in favor of the court decision allowing Swanson to attend UVA, the university's president, Colgate Darden, privately wrote that Swanson's admission undermined southern traditions and Jeffersonian ideals.

As a result of Swanson's legal effort, however, Black students were able to attend the other state schools, including the historic College of William & Mary, as long as Virginia State didn't offer the same program.

Despite such small advances, the Encyclopedia Virginia noted, Virginia universities "remained segregated institutions into the 1960s." Even the few Black students who did get in found life very restrictive, especially housing. Black engineering students at Virginia Polytechnic University (now Virginia Tech) had to live off campus. At UVA and VPI, Black athletes couldn't play varsity athletics until the 1960s.

The Southeastern Conference (SEC), long a powerhouse on the gridiron, refused to let Blacks compete on its sports teams and often even refused to play schools that fielded Black athletes. In the face of the burgeoning Civil Rights Movement in 1956, Louisiana passed a law banning interracial sports competition. The Supreme Court rejected it three years later. Facing a cutoff of state funds for playing against interracial squads, Mississippi State didn't play in the NCAA basketball tournament in 1959, 1961 and 1962.

The first two Black football players finally suited up for Kentucky in 1966. In fact, not until 1971 did every SEC team have at least one Black athlete.

By comparison, Ivy League schools in the 1800s featured a few Black athletes, such as William Edward White, who played on Brown's 1879 baseball team. William Henry Lewis achieved All-America football status at Harvard in 1892. Other universities followed suit. Preston Eagleson starred in football at Indiana University in the 1890s. Other Black athletes dotted rosters at the University of Wisconsin and Michigan State, according to a report by ESPN's Richard Lapchick in 2008.

Harris was already thirty when the Supreme Court finally stepped in by ending "separate but equal" educational systems with its 1954 ruling in the case of *Brown v. Topeka Board of Education*. In it, the Supreme Court ended the "separate but equal" condition in place since 1896. The case will be discussed further in the next chapter.

The Supreme Court's ruling did not exactly go over well in Virginia. Schools were authorized to close rather than to accept the ruling. Many did. Prince Edward County schools shut down for years to protest the decision. Charlottesville and Albemarle County schools followed Prince Edward's lead for a shorter duration, while the state legislature declared the Supreme Court decision null and void. Facing infuriated parents, many schools reopened very quickly. However, Prince Edward County did not unlock school doors until forced to by federal courts.

For Harris, then, segregated schools and Black-only universities were his lone options.

That was the world Harris knew, one dominated by intense hatred based simply on the color of a person's skin. Nothing would change that attitude until the Civil Rights Movement began to bubble in the 1950s. By then, Harris had reached the apparent peak of his employment opportunities in Virginia. He was a janitor.

CHAPTER 4

WORKING

FIRST DEMONSTRATION, MONTGOMERY BOYCOTT, LIFE IN HOPEWELL

After graduating from high school, Harris went to work for the Hercules Powder Company, which was founded in 1912 from the remnants of the E.I. DuPont de Nemours and Company. DuPont had gobbled up a variety of chemical companies in the preceding years. Under the Sherman Anti-Trust Act, which ended monopolies in oil and other fields, the government ordered the big chemical firm to get rid of some of its holdings. Hercules was one of the discarded businesses.

At first, Hercules made blasting powder and dynamite, black powder and smokeless powder, supplying the Allies with explosives and propellants during World War I. In 1926, the company bought Virginia Cellulose of Hopewell, which made cotton linters. By the time Harris joined the company, Hercules's Virginia plant was the leading supplier of cellulose for the chemical industry.

The janitorial work was unfulfilling. Harris finally convinced his older sister to pay his tuition at Virginia Union University (VUU) in Richmond. Money for tuition came from the restaurant. He enrolled in religious studies at the school, which was founded days after Richmond fell to the Union army in 1865 with the goal of educating freed Black men interested in becoming Baptist ministers. Its mission quickly expanded to encompass other aspects of education. One alumnus, Lyman T. Johnson, integrated the University of Kentucky in 1930.

When Harris actually went to VUU is unclear. He would have graduated high school in 1941. Based on his recollections, he attended VUU in 1945

The home of Rev.
Curtis and Ruth
Harris in Hopewell.
*Courtesy of Jeremy
M. Lazarus.*

and 1946. However, in a published statement, Harris said he attended VUU in 1954. Later, Harris earned a certificate in clinical training for pastors from the Medical College of Virginia and studied at the Urban Training Center for Christian Missions in Chicago, Illinois.

Harris stayed at VUU for two years before marrying Ruth Jones, whom he had met at Woodson. Harris said, "I noticed her in high school," while they both were dancing in the weekly talent program in the school. "I could really cut a rug then," he said.

Harris really had no thoughts about his future. Ruth, however, was highly motivated. To get an education, she walked three miles every day to Woodson. Her parents expected her to go to college. She earned money in the time-honored ways: babysitting and cleaning homes.

The eldest of six children, Ruth was born in Dendron on February 1, 1925. Two years later, her parents, Daniel and Novella Jones, moved the family to Hopewell to seek better jobs—joining the growing number of migrants that included Curtis Harris and his siblings. Ruth was elected president of her high school senior class at Carter G. Woodson, one year after her future husband graduated. She then received a certificate from the Virginia State College of Beauty Culture and Cosmetology and later studied social work at Virginia Union University. She also took business administration and early childhood development courses at Virginia State University.

In 1953, she opened the Harris and Young Beauty Salon. In 1959, she turned to the restaurant business with her husband, starting up the Harris Snack Bar. Ruth was manager and head cook. The little diner quickly became a community landmark and meeting place of Black activists. Dr. Martin Luther King Jr. stopped in during one of his visits there in the early 1960s. In 1972, Ruth founded the Union Day Care Center.

The small store run by Ruth Harris near the Harris home in Hopewell. *Courtesy of Jeremy M. Lazarus.*

For Harris, however, the main role for the woman eventually known as "Mrs. Ruth" was to continually encourage him. "I realize now more than at the time that she must have had some sleepless nights," Harris said. "She was praying for me and the others. That was a very important factor in my life. I couldn't function too much without her. I couldn't even button up my shirt. She was my right arm."

At her funeral in 2011, Andrew Shannon, chapter president of the Southern Christian Leadership Conference (SCLC) in Newport News and vice president of the state SCLC, said of Ruth, "She was a quiet warrior. She was a force who supported Dr. Harris. When she saw that something was wrong, she would take a stand."

Curtis and Ruth were married for sixty-five years and had six children: Curtis Jr., Kenneth, Michael, Joanne, Karen and Michelle.

For his family, as for Harris, religion was the touchstone. Harris would quote lines from Psalm 121 and required his children to memorize it. "I will lift up mine eyes unto the hills, from whence comes my help, and where it comes from, knowing that it doesn't come from that mountain, it comes from who made the mountain," he recited.

Early in their marriage, Ruth and Curtis lived in Norfolk, which was then, as now, a military center and major port. Within a few years, the couple returned to Hopewell, where Curtis Harris found a menial job at Allied Chemical. "With my two years of college, you would assume that I would get a job better than a janitor, but the rule was that you could not take a job beyond a janitor. You couldn't be a truck driver, you couldn't be a mechanic, you couldn't be anything beyond a janitor," Harris said.

Harris knew full well why, too. "It was a racial discrimination situation," he continued. "I knew that when I took the job because I had to have a job. By this time, I am married, and I had to feed my family. So, I was working, and I worked there for 15 years and—but I was always conscious of the discrimination that was going on, and I was not able to do anything." The situation galled him. "My mother accepted it," he recalled. "She was a domestic, and she worked for white people. Because we didn't have much, she used to bring home leftovers from the white folk table and hand-me-downs from the clothes that we had to wear. But I never accepted it."

Harris said, "I guess my position is that I am a person who looks at life and deals with it on the spot. There's always something that I have to do to function, and I believe the Lord helps me do it."

The racial situation at Allied was not different from other Virginia companies, just more obvious because of its size. Founded in the 1920s when five chemical plants merged and moved into the old DuPont facility in Hopewell, the company had become a local behemoth. It initially produced synthetic ammonia, becoming the world leader in that field.

Through several name changes, it continued to expand into a variety of areas, including synthetic nitrogen, which was vital during World War II, as well as oil and gas exploration and aerospace. Today known as Honeywell International, the company also had a reputation for being extremely conservative in its attitude and secretive. Although employing thousands of workers, into the 1960s, it maintained the Virginia tradition of segregation of Black and white employees, while restricting Blacks to low-level positions.

While working, Harris continued his religious activities. In 1956, he was licensed as a minister in the Baptist faith in ceremonies conducted by Union Baptist Church pastor Dr. George Washington King. "I learned a lot from him," Harris said. Three years later, he would replace the ailing Dr. King as pastor of the church.

By then, Harris had begun his civil rights efforts. He credits his mother for inspiring him. "My mother was a mild-mannered lady, but she didn't take no stuff. I think I must have taken after her. I never had a father, and she was always helping folks (although) we didn't have anything. We were just as poor as we could be, but she taught me how to share. I think that's what brought me to my involvement in the Civil Rights Movement," he said.

His wife had something to do with it, too. Ruth attended a local meeting for wives interested in starting a Boy Scouts troop. There had been a troop before, Harris said, but there was interest in starting another one. Ruth volunteered her husband to be scoutmaster.

"I didn't know anything about scouting," Harris admitted, but he had no hesitancy to

INSTALLATION SERVICES
of
CURTIS WEST HARRIS

PASTOR-ELECT
Union Baptist Church
Hopewell, Virginia

October 23-27, 1961, 8:00 P. M.
(Night of October 28th excepted)

CLOSING SERVICE:
Sunday, October 29, 1961
4:00 P. M.

The pamphlet announcing Rev. Curtis W. Harris's installation as minister of the Union Baptist Church in Hopewell. *Courtesy of Swem Library, College of William & Mary.*

step to the front. His wife never felt comfortable as a public speaker, but not Harris. "Before I was 10," he said, "when someone would fight, I'd lead the fight. People began to look to me for leadership. I didn't know what was going on, why people were looking at me that way, but that was my time."

In the 1950s, while a scoutmaster, Harris began his battles on a bigger stage. Naturally, his first target was Allied. Harris had been elected union shop steward there and actively pushed the company to promote African Americans. "We thought that Black people ought to have the opportunity to go into higher positions," he said.

His efforts were largely ignored until President John F. Kennedy issued Executive Order 10925 in 1961, requiring all companies that received federal contracts to end hiring discrimination practices. According to the order, companies must "take affirmative action to ensure that applicants are employed and that employees are treated during employment without regard to their race, creed, color, or national origin."

The order also created the Committee on Equal Employment Opportunity and put the words "affirmative action" into the American lexicon. Kennedy's successor, Lyndon Johnson, emphasized his call for the end of discrimination as part of speech given at Howard University, a historically Black institution in Washington, D.C. Johnson said:

> *But freedom is not enough. You do not wipe away the scars of centuries by saying: Now you are free to go where you want, and do as you desire, and choose the leaders you please. You do not take a person who, for years, has been hobbled by chains and liberate him, bring him up to the starting line of a race and then say, "You are free to compete with all the others," and still justly believe that you have been completely fair. Thus, it is not enough just to open the gates of opportunity. All our citizens must have the ability to walk through those gates.*
>
> *This is the next and the more profound stage of the battle for civil rights. We seek not just freedom but opportunity. We seek not just legal equity but human ability, not just equality as a right and a theory but equality as a fact and equality as a result. For the task is to give 20 million Negroes the same chance as every other American to learn and grow, to work and share in society, to develop their abilities—physical, mental and spiritual, and to pursue their individual happiness.*

Under federal pressure, Allied had to comply but did so unwillingly. Harris found out about the president's action and knew Allied had government contracts. When the company refused to follow the president's directive, he filed suit. "I had enough to threaten them," Harris said. "They thought I knew more than I knew."

His lawyers were the most prominent Black attorneys in the area: Oliver Hill, Henry L. Marsh III and Samuel W. Tucker. Hill, who died in 2007, served as the chairman of the NAACP's Virginia legal staff. The Virginia native is credited with filing more legal challenges to racial laws than any other southern attorney. He later received the Presidential Medal of Freedom in 1999 after helping win cases involving equality in pay for Black teachers, jury selection and voting rights, among other issues. Hill joined with Spottswood Robinson III to file the lawsuit that became one of the five cases that made up *Brown v. Topeka Board of Education*, the case that ended the "separate but equal" limitations in American society.

Robinson, a native Virginian who died in 1998, later served as dean of the Howard University Law School and chief judge of the United States Circuit Court of Appeals for the District of Columbia.

Marsh, who was born in Richmond but raised in West Virginia, helped end Richmond's segregated educational system. He was later Richmond's first African American mayor and served as a state senator. Tucker, who was born in Alexandria, Virginia, sued Richmond to equalize Black teachers' salaries with their white counterparts. Later, he joined a lawsuit that forced Richmond to desegregate the school faculty, special programs for disabled and gifted students and adult programs. He died in 1990.

Harris's Allied case took a while to wind through the courts, but eventually, the plaintiffs were awarded $250,000 for discrimination. In addition, the company allowed African Americans to move into other jobs in the plant, Harris said, including truck drivers, operators and corporate officials. "Finally, they hired a couple of African-American women in the main office as secretaries," he noted.

By the time the Allied case was settled, Harris had left the company. In 1959, he had become pastor of Union Baptist Church, a position he would hold for the next fifty years. His wife ran the children's program there. As a former employee of Allied, Harris didn't figure to receive any of the settlement cash, but the lawyers brought checks to the church, he recalled. The money was distributed there by James W. Benton Jr., who would become the state's first Black supreme court judge. "Some people didn't know about it ahead of time," Harris said. "They had to go to the attorneys' office to get their check."

The case was part of a rise in Black demands for civil rights that were fueled by a variety of cultural trends. For one thing, southern states had begun to move away from an agricultural base to an industrial one. The former slave families who had stayed on plantations as tenant farmers lost jobs as machinery took over. Chronically unemployed, Black laborers swarmed into cities to find work in factories, much as Harris did. The economics began to outweigh any animosities. To grow, many companies realized that the old Jim Crow laws deterred investors. Lynching had an even worse impact. Behind the scenes, corporate leaders moved to ease racial restrictions as an effort to boost financial opportunities.

In addition, economic restraints after World War II forced countries like England, France and Portugal to end colonial rule in Africa. As African nations formed, American Blacks saw native leaders become heads of government. They began to question their own roles in an American society that did not allow them to vote or achieve more than modest levels of success.

The final push came from national leaders, beginning in 1948. That year, President Harry Truman issued Executive Order 9981, ending racial segregation in the military, one year after Jackie Robinson broke the unwritten color barrier in professional baseball, then the nation's foremost sport.

The Union
Baptist Church
in Hopewell
where Rev.
Curtis W. Harris
Sr. served as
pastor from
1959 to 2007.
*Courtesy of Jeremy
M. Lazarus.*

The necessary legal support came in 1954 with *Brown v. the Board of Education of Topeka,* a U.S. Supreme Court ruling that outlawed the separate but equal criteria. The case involved a third grader who had to walk a mile through a railroad junction to reach her Black elementary school, even though a white elementary school was only seven blocks away.

The case drew widespread interest and created a scenario of dueling specialists. The head of the University of Kansas Department of Education, Dr. Hugh W. Speer, testified that "if the colored children are denied the experience in school of associating with white children, who represent 90 percent of our national society in which these colored children must live, then the colored child's curriculum is being greatly curtailed. The Topeka curriculum or any school curriculum cannot be equal under segregation." The board of education countered that segregation in Topeka prepared Black children for the same restrictions in the real world.

The board won the case initially because of the precedent of *Plessy v. Ferguson*, even though the U.S. district court agreed that "segregation of white and colored children in public schools has a detrimental effect upon the colored children….A sense of inferiority affects the motivation of a child to learn."

The case eventually reached the U.S. Supreme Court, which unanimously struck down the law. "Separate educational facilities are inherently unequal," Chief Justice Earl Warren announced in the 1954 decision that overturned *Plessy v. Ferguson*.

Harris was president of the PTA at Carter G. Woodson High School that year. The organization was trying to recruit Blacks into teaching despite low pay. During a PTA meeting, someone whispered for him to come outside, Harris recalled. That's when he learned that the Supreme Court had outlawed segregation. "When I came back," Harris continued, "I stopped the meeting, so I could make the announcement. The white people there didn't know whether to laugh or say, 'I'm sorry,' but the Black people were rejoicing."

Changes in society helped support the court's wide-ranging decision. Initially, the U.S. government was involved in desperate struggles during World War II against Nazi aggression and then in a lengthy Cold War against the Soviet Union and its dictatorial policies. The idea that Americans stood for freedom and justice paled when compared with the United States' domestic record of segregation and racism. Government and industry leaders realized that America's treatment of Blacks had created an indelible stain on this country's reputation abroad. Soviet communist leaders regularly pointed to the second-class treatment of Black Americans to dig at the United States' claims of being a leader of the free world. Kennedy's executive order was designed to counter those charges. Presidents Lyndon Johnson and Richard Nixon later added additional orders to enhance the effort.

While the federal government slowly began to move against racism, an event occurred that would engender the Civil Rights Movement, a social current that would dominate Harris's life for the next five decades.

One year after the momentous *Brown v. Topeka Board of Education* ruling, a weary seamstress employed by the Montgomery Fair department store refused to move to the back of a Montgomery, Alabama bus. Rosa Parks, who was later labeled "the Mother of the Civil Rights Movement," climbed aboard a Cleveland Avenue bus to go home on December 1, 1955. She sat in the area reserved for Blacks and then declined to surrender her seat to a late-arriving white man.

That was a violation of the Montgomery city code that required that all public transportation be segregated and gave bus drivers the "powers of a police officer of the city while in actual charge of any bus for the purposes of carrying out the provisions" of the code. While operating a bus, drivers were mandated to assign seats to enforce separate but equal accommodations for white and Black passengers. Each bus had a sign placed roughly in the middle of the bus to separate the front white section from the rear Black area. If too many whites entered, the driver would shift the sign toward the back of the bus and require Black passengers to give up their seats.

When Parks, like all Black riders, entered the bus, she was obligated to pay in front, exit and reenter through the rear door. She did. However, when excess white passengers boarded the bus and the sign was relocated, she insisted on staying in what had become a white-only section.

"Our mistreatment was just not right, and I was tired of it," Parks wrote in her 1994 book *Quiet Strength*. "I kept thinking about my mother and my grandparents, and how strong they were. I knew there was a possibility of being mistreated, but an opportunity was being given to me to do what I had asked of others."

Parks, who died in 2005, was already an activist and served as secretary of the NAACP. She had previously attempted unsuccessfully to register to vote on several occasions. She had also grown up with racism. "Back then," she told an interviewer, "we didn't have any civil rights. It was just a matter of survival, of existing from one day to the next. I remember going to sleep as a girl hearing the Klan ride at night and hearing a lynching and being afraid the house would burn down."

After she declined to move, although three other Black passengers did, the bus driver called police. Parks was arrested for disorderly conduct and for violating a local ordinance. She was fined ten dollars plus four dollars in court costs. "I didn't have any special fear," she said. Instead, as the community rallied behind her, she began to feel encouraged. "It was more of a relief to know that I wasn't alone," she said.

As with Daniel Desdunes and Homer Plessy in Louisiana some sixty years earlier, Parks had wittingly become involved in a test case. The lawsuit really originated in 1949 when Jo Ann Robinson, a Black Alabama State College professor, sat in the wrong section of a bus and was chased off by an angry driver. Robinson then joined the Women's Political Council, a group that was designed to motivate African American women to take political action and later spearhead the Montgomery boycott. Several years after Robinson ran off the bus in tears, local pastor Vernon Johns tried to get other Blacks to leave a bus to protest the law without garnering any support.

Long active in civil rights efforts, Johns preceded Dr. Martin Luther King Jr. as pastor of Dexter Avenue Baptist Church. Known for having a photographic memory and for unsuccessfully holding a one-man sit-in, Johns died in 1965.

At the time of her 1949 incident, Robinson also called for a boycott, with no success. Other groups did the same thing, with minimal public response.

By 1955, however, enough Black civic organizations were emboldened by the *Brown v. Board of Education* ruling and sufficiently outraged to begin searching for the right person to serve as the defendant. They needed someone beyond reproach, said Edgar Daniel Nixon, then head of the Montgomery branch of the Pullman Porters union and president of the local NAACP chapter. Already an activist, Nixon had been working to get Black residents registered to vote. At one point back in 1940, he had led a group of 750 men to the Montgomery County courthouse to attempt to register. Probably as a sarcastic gesture, a year before the Parks incident, he had run unsuccessfully for a seat on the county Democratic Party executive committee.

Nixon thought Claudette Colvin, age fifteen, would be the ideal defendant when she was arrested in March 1955 for sitting in the wrong seat on the same bus Rosa Parks would ride nine months later. Then a high school student, Colvin said that nothing specific prompted her to remain in her seat as the bus filled with white riders, according to a *Montgomery Advertiser* newspaper interview conducted years later. Actually, she may have been thinking about a high school essay she had written that day, which complained that Black Montgomery residents were unable to use dressing rooms in local department stores to try on clothes.

Asked by the driver to move when two white women were forced to stand, she adamantly declined. Two other Black passengers did relocate but not Colvin, who later became a nurse's aide and moved to New York City. "I just said I am not going to take this anymore," Colvin said. "I was not breaking the law." A classmate said Colvin yelled, "It's my Constitutional right."

Colvin said police tossed her schoolbooks from the bus. Then, two officers grabbed her arms and dragged her off. She was later convicted of violating the law and assaulting a police officer. However, she was not used in the test case. Colvin was supposedly pregnant and soon dropped out of school—hardly the "pure" candidate Nixon wanted for a lawsuit. Actually, according to published accounts, Colvin did not become pregnant until after the incident. She later testified in the lawsuit that eventually ended segregation on Alabama buses, although she said the resulting notoriety affected her career opportunities.

In 2017, Colvin was finally recognized when March 2 was declared Claudette Colvin Day in Montgomery. "Young people think Rosa Parks just sat down on a bus and ended segregation, but that wasn't the case at all," Colvin said.

Nevertheless, Nixon went looking for someone else. A friend called to tell him about the arrest of Parks, who had attended Alabama State, was aware of the Colvin case and had recently participated in a workshop on race relations. With white supporters Clifford and Virginia Durr, Nixon bailed her out of jail and asked her to serve as the test. She agreed. Later, organizers said that Parks, then forty-two, "would be a better test case for integration because she was an adult and had the kind of hair and appearance needed to make her look middle class."

Colvin later said she was not unhappy Parks was chosen, just disappointed. In a 2005 interview published in the *Montgomery Advertiser*, Colvin said she would not have changed her decision to remain seated on the bus even if given the chance. "I feel very, very proud of what I did," she said. "I do feel like what I did was a spark and it caught on."

The fire spread across the city. Overnight, Robinson produced fifty thousand handouts calling for a one-day boycott the following Monday, the day Parks was to face the judge. The sheets proclaimed: "People, don't ride the bus today. Don't ride it for Freedom." Few thought the idea would have much success.

The Reverend Martin Luther King Jr., then the unknown minister of the Dexter Avenue Baptist Church, wrote that he thought "if we could get 60 percent cooperation, the protest would be a success." On Monday morning, however, an empty bus rolled by his house. "A miracle had taken place," King later recorded. "The once dormant and quiescent Negro community was now fully awake."

That afternoon, the Black leaders met and decided to name themselves the Montgomery Improvement Association (MIA). King was elected president, launching his national career and shunting a resentful Nixon to the sidelines. The Reverend Ralph David Abernathy, who would eventually succeed King as the face of the Civil Rights Movement, was the program director. The two men met in 1954 when both were pastors of nearby churches. Then, the group voted unanimously to continue the boycott, which was not an uncommon protest tactic. A boycott in Baton

Rouge several years earlier had reduced segregation—separate sections of bus seats were reserved for both Black and white riders.

The MIA had more success. An estimated 90 percent of Montgomery's Black riders stayed off the buses, reducing company revue by more than 75 percent. Black riders walked or arranged carpools, sometimes with the help of sympathetic white residents and Black leaders like King.

Parks coordinated rides for boycott participants and was later indicted for her involvement in that facet of the protest. So was King, along with eighty-seven other Blacks, under an old law banning boycotts. King went on trial first and was fined $500 with an additional $500 tacked on in court costs. If he didn't write a check, he faced a year in jail. He eventually paid the fine.

There were plenty of fines. Professor Robinson noted that many unemployed employees of now-defunct bus companies were hired as policemen. She reported that "many of those policemen would give just hundreds and hundreds of tickets every day to Black people who were not violating any traffic laws, but they were doing it to help the salaries they had lost." She also watched two policemen pour gas over her car. Robinson was named to the MIA's executive board and produced the organization's weekly newsletter. She later moved to California and, in 1987, produced a memoir titled *The Montgomery Bus Boycott and the Woman Who Started It*. She died in 1992.

Despite the harassment faced by organizers and participants, the boycott continued and lasted more than a year—far exceeding the single day Robinson called for—with widespread support, as a poignant anecdote emphasizes:

> *One white bus driver stopped to let off a lone black man in a black neighborhood. Looking in his rearview mirror, he saw an old black woman with a cane rushing towards the bus. He opened the door and said, "You don't have to rush, auntie. I'll wait for you." The woman replied, "In the first place, I ain't your auntie. In the second place, I ain't rushing to get on your bus. I'm jus' trying to catch up with that nigger who just got off, so I can hit him with this here stick."*

For eleven months, the bus company struggled to survive with financial support from the racist Ku Klux Klan and the Citizens' Council, a white group formed to oppose integration. Then, in November 1956, the U.S. Supreme Court overturned the law allowing segregation on city buses. The company finally conceded, the boycott ended and the buses resumed their normal routine on December 21, 1956.

However, the entire community did not embrace desegregated rides. Buses were shot at. For safety reasons, the city stopped bus service after five o'clock, so shooters would not have the cover of night. A whites-only bus service started and failed. Bombs were set off near the homes of three Black families and four Baptist churches, among other places. Abernathy's home and church were on that list. King's home would have gone up in smoke, too, but a bomb placed on his porch failed to explode. Robinson's home needed twenty-four-hour police protection.

Five men were indicted for the violence, but no one was convicted, despite two signed confessions. The others were freed in exchange for allowing Blacks charged under the boycott law to walk away, according to Missouri teacher Lisa Cozzens in her lengthy report on the Civil Rights Movement between 1955 and 1965.

The Montgomery boycott was actually not a large event, but, according to author Roberta Hughes Wright in her 1991 book *The Birth of the Montgomery Bus Boycott*, "It helped to launch a 10-year national struggle for freedom and justice, the Civil Rights Movement, that stimulated others to do the same at home and abroad."

The events in Montgomery also introduced activitists to the idea that going to jail was part of the battle. For community leaders, prisons filled social and political roles by hiding troublemakers from public view. To them, justice could operate better if activities undertaken in prison were kept hidden.

As a result, after Parks was arrested, King was next in line. For the first time in his life, he was taken to jail. At the same time, he told Black ministers and civic leaders gathered in the city to be ready to follow him. Like him, other activists began to realize that breaking the law served a greater good and that time in jail was a necessary sacrifice.

There would be plenty of opportunities to prove that. Southern states fought back, ignoring court decisions. Finally, in 1957, three years after the *Brown v. Topeka Board of Education* ruling, the Supreme Court required the Little Rock, Arkansas school district to desegregate its schools. Arkansas governor Orval Faubus objected, saying states had the right to run their own schools. His argument smacked of the justification for the Civil War: states' rights versus the federal government.

Faubus created a confrontation by ordering the state national guard to block nine Black students from entering Little Rock High School that year. The resulting confrontation was televised. Americans watched troops form a thicket with their bayonets to keep the youngsters from entering the school. President Dwight Eisenhower sent in federal troops to force integration, but white mobs surrounded the school, attacking and threatening the children. Little Rock schools shut down for a year before reopening to limited integration.

The only winner was Faubus, who had been, ironically, known as a racial moderate prior to this traumatic event and who was promptly reelected four more times. To date, he remains the longest serving of all Arkansas governors.

These scenes in Arkansas would be repeated at other bastions of racism, most notably at the University of Mississippi in 1962.

Nevertheless, the Civil Rights Movement was underway. The events in Montgomery certainly galvanized Harris, who would lead boycotts, face off against the KKK and angry whites and be invited to enjoy the dubious pleasures of local jails. Perhaps encouraged by activists' success in far-off Alabama or simply energized by the events, he began to plan and organize against the forces of racism in tiny Hopewell and throughout Virginia.

Harris was up against ingrained hatred in Hopewell. Harris's eldest son, Curtis Jr., spelled out the situation in a letter published in 2017. He was responding to an essay by Joan Holland, who writes a weekly column for a local publication.

I would like to publicly address Ms. Joan Holland's "Commentary" printed by your newspaper a few weeks ago (do not know exact date). In that commentary, Ms. Holland expressed her desire to return to the "old days" of Hopewell.

My name is Curtis W. Harris Jr. and I grew up in Hopewell. I attended Carter G. Woodson High School (through the 11th grade), and Hopewell High School (in 12th grade, graduating in 1964).

Curtis Jr. then supplied his own commentary that "expresses my concern with Ms. Holland's depiction of Hopewell in the 'old days.'"

The "old days" in Hopewell were not as joyous for me and my family as they were for Joan Holland. In her "commentary" of several weeks ago, she elaborated on how wonderful the retail establishments in downtown were for the "people" of Hopewell. She also mentioned recreational facilities such as Moore's Lake, Crystal Lake, and Red Water Lake and their popularity, as well as how the "people" loved them.

The retail establishments she mentioned by name, which included George's Drug Stores (Numbers 1 and 2), Woolworth's and W.T. Grants, as well as many other eating establishments, routinely discriminated against a large portion of the citizenry of Hopewell denying them entry into their establishments, or, if they were allowed entry, refusing to let them sit and eat on the premises.

My mother could buy clothes at a number of the women's shops Ms. Holland wrote about, but, unlike the white women, she was not allowed to try them on before she purchased them.

The "wonderful" movies playing at the Beacon Theatre and the Park Drive-In were for white citizens only.

Today, politicians and writers such as Ms. Holland talk about returning to the "old days," as though the persons who were discriminated against would enjoy returning to a time of riding in the back of the bus, drinking out of separate water fountains, and being refused admission to public facilities such as the library, the city cemetery, and the so-called public pool in City Point.

I will also never forget having to go into the backdoor of doctor's offices and using a separate entrance to the bus station. On the occasions when we visited the Bellwood Drive-In on Route One, I would wonder why the white children had all kinds of recreational equipment to play with at the front of the drive-in, while we had no recreational equipment to play with in the segregated section for blacks, which was in the far back rows of the drive-in.

As a young child, my parents insisted on the city allowing us to swim in the public pool located in City Point. Rather than allowing all of its citizens to enjoy the cool waters of the tax-supported, city-owned facility, the decision was made to fill the pool with cement. Eventually, the recreation department replaced the pool with two tennis courts, so my father bought me and my brother tennis racquets. I became a good player, and participated in many tennis tournaments in Virginia, Maryland and Washington, DC.

During my time studying music at Carter G. Woodson High School, the materials provided by the Board of Education for the Music Department were very inadequate. The Instrumental Music Program only survived because of the dedicated work of teachers such as Mr. Maclin, Mr. Taylor, Mr. Bellamy and Mr. Hall. One year, Hopewell High School received new band uniforms and gave their "discarded" uniforms to Woodson.

Unfortunately, they only gave the school twenty uniforms, despite the fact that there were about fifty members in the Woodson Marching Band. I was one of the "fortunate" members who received a blue and gold tattered uniform, even though our school colors were maroon and gray. The rest of the band wore white pants and shirts.

In 1963, as the result of a court order, I transferred to Hopewell High and was surprised by the number of extra-curricular activities offered to allow for a complete educational experience for the students. At Woodson, the only sports offered were basketball and baseball, but at Hopewell High, a full array of sports teams were a part of the school's extra-curricular activities (basketball [boys and girls], baseball, track, volleyball, etc.).

At Woodson, the music program included band and chorus, however, both programs were poorly funded, which resulted in the inability of the music teachers to have the programs reach their full potential. In contrast, Hopewell High had several types of vocal groups and a large instrumental program that allowed students to perform at football games and venues outside of the city. Despite the inequities between Woodson and Hopewell High, and the demeaning treatment I received at Hopewell High, I became a band director and taught school for 35 years.

Included in my remarks are just a few of the advantages white citizens of Hopewell enjoyed that were denied to its African-American residents.

The last paragraph of Ms. Holland's commentary, where she talked about "old times seeming like a dream," caused me to understand why there is still such a racial divide in our country today. While white citizens of Hopewell talk about the old days as a "dream that exists only in the pleasant past," I remember having a bomb thrown into my home, and, later, into my parent's restaurant next door to our home.

While Ms. Holland wants a return to those times, my thoughts are of a burning cross placed in my front yard, and of insulting notes and ugly drawings being placed in my school desk at Hopewell High.

I long for uplifting discussions on those "old days" to determine why those times had to happen, and positive ways to ensure that no group will ever have to endure the discriminatory practices of that era. Discussions along these lines should help curb commentaries, such as Ms. Holland's, that continue to be insensitive to certain citizens of Hopewell.

As an adult, Curtis Jr. also was able to see the many changes that took place in Hopewell's racial policies, many of which his father forced on a reluctant community.

CHAPTER 5

CONFLICT

SIT-INS AND LEGAL BATTLES, KKK CONFRONTATION, ETHANOL PLANT

H arris actually had a base to work from when he launched his various actions against Hopewell's racist white leadership. In 1950, he had been named president of the NAACP's branch in Hopewell. It wasn't a commitment of any sort. Harris recalled that a Black doctor in town, C.A. Robbins, and another unidentified man headed the local chapter, which had been in Hopewell since at least World War II. The national organization was far older, having been founded after a race riot in Springfield, Illinois, in 1908.

That riot began on August 14 when white residents found that the local sheriff had relocated two young Black men charged with rape and murder to an out-of-town jail. In the resulting three days of tumult, state militia killed five people, while another eleven died. Overall, nine Blacks were killed amid more than $1 million worth of damages. Several stores were burned, including three owned by whites thought to be sympathetic to Blacks.

The horrific events galvanized Black leaders, who, on February 12, 1909, the centennial of Lincoln's birth, called for the creation of a national organization to fight such outrages. In May, dozens of people gathered in New York to establish the NAACP with the stated goal of securing "for all people the rights guaranteed in the 13th, 14th, and 15th Amendments to the United States Constitution, which promised an end to slavery, the equal protection of the law, and universal adult male suffrage, respectively." New York became the group's headquarters a year later.

The NAACP quickly launched legal campaigns against discriminatory laws and fought lynching. As a result, it expanded to include some three hundred local branches by 1919. By 1946, membership rolls swelled to around six hundred thousand as Black soldiers, returning from fighting for their country beside their white counterparts, demanded equality.

Four years later, Harris found himself an official in the organization. "When they were looking for someone to take over the NAACP," he said, "they selected me in my absence. There were no (other) young folk in the movement." Harris was twenty-six years old.

Harris joined only to follow his wife, according to their daughter Joanne. She said her mom came home late one night. Harris was upset and wanted to know where Ruth had been. She told him that she had gone to a NAACP meeting. After that, he started attending, Joanne said. Harris probably didn't expect to do much as president because he knew that the NAACP in Hopewell was not the activist group it would become in the 1960s.

"What we were doing for the most part," Harris said, "was talking about the conditions. We weren't involved in no cases up to that time." Members were aware of what was happening elsewhere, such as court decisions, but were not particularly motivated to do anything about it locally. Not even the momentous *Brown v. the Topeka Board of Education* decision fired up the complacent group. For the local NAACP, the ruling was simply grist for conversations. "When something came up, we would wear that out until the next thing happened," Harris recalled. "Nothing was happening in Hopewell. As long as nothing was happening in Hopewell, we were home free."

That changed after Montgomery. Even in Hopewell, Harris began to see a modest thaw in race relations. There were meetings between some white people and Black people, he said. The slow change in Virginia had begun in Richmond with the founding of the Council on Human Relations by the Reverend Heslip "Happy" Lee, a white minister who advocated for civil justice. Lee, who died in 2011, had been born to a tenant farmer in rural Georgia. After graduating from Colgate Rochester Divinity School, he became involved in the Civil Rights Movement and served as executive director of the Virginia Council on Human Relations. He said his finest moment came when he helped orchestrate the reopening of public schools in Prince Edward County, Virginia, in 1964, five years after they closed rather than desegregate.

Lee and Harris got along well, both because of their comparative religious backgrounds and their ideology. Lee said, "I spent my entire life fighting three things: poverty, racism and fun DA Mentalism [*sic*]," which

VIRGINIA'S CIVIL RIGHTS HERO CURTIS W. HARRIS SR.

he defined as "those people who damn others for having religious beliefs different from their own."

Some white Hopewell residents became aware of the Council on Human Relations and began to gather in small local meetings. Harris recalls participants as being educated professionals. "They were college people," he said. "One was a nurse, and one was a college engineer. What they were trying to do, I think, was to improve the relationships. They were also deeply religious."

Harris didn't expect overnight shifts in racial attitudes. "It was a gradual process, and they were people who previously had some relationship with some African-Americans for some reason or another," he said. The racism faced by Black residents disturbed them. "It was really embarrassing for some of the whites to see what was happening," he said.

Harris didn't care how red-faced they were. He was about to add to the headlines. He started by cofounding the Hopewell Improvement Association (HIA), which became a chapter of fledgling Southern Christian Leadership Conference (SCLC). Dr. Martin Luther King Jr. had helped form the SCLC in 1957 as an amalgamation of various antiracism groups. He invited some sixty black ministers and leaders to Atlanta. Among those who attended were Bayard Rustin, who first suggested the idea a year before; the Reverend Fred Shuttlesworth of Montgomery; the Reverend Joseph Lowery of Mobile; the Reverend Ralph Abernathy of Montgomery; and the Reverend C.K. Steele of Tallahassee. A follow-up meeting in New Orleans ended with King being elected president of the Negro Leaders Conference on Nonviolent Integration. That was changed to the Southern Negro Leaders Conference before becoming the SCLC, with an office in Atlanta. The group grew by creating affiliates, in contrast to other civil rights groups that expanded by recruiting individuals to set up local chapters.

Once in place, the SCLC began to initiate boycotts throughout the South like the one that had worked in Montgomery. Besides calling on white Americans to join in the struggle against racism, the SCLC encouraged Black Americans "seek justice and reject all injustice, but to do so nonviolently." The SCLC publicly insisted that "not one hair of one head of one white person shall be harmed," while helping Blacks register to vote and open desegregated schools. At the same time, its message was that civil rights had to be seen as a moral issue, an idea emphasized by the use of "Christian" in its name.

Harris quickly recognized the value of affiliating with the SCLC and, in 1961, joined the board of the national organization. The group's religious overtone suited his own feelings and matched those within the Black community. Dr. Martin Luther King Jr.'s involvement helped, too. "When the sit-in movement started, Dr. King became my mentor," Harris said. "He was mild-mannered, but he had a charisma that was out of this world."

As a result, the local HIA was modeled on the activist group that led the successful boycott in Montgomery. The tiny organization also quickly became part of a national movement headed by the Reverend Dr. Wyatt Tee Walker, a resident of nearby Petersburg and later head of the Southern Christian Leadership Conference. He joined the group in 1961 and spent three years as executive director, developing a structured fundraising strategy and organizing numerous protests, including a series of anti-segregation boycotts and demonstrations in Birmingham, Alabama. His strategy became the model for similar protests across the South.

Known as King's right-hand man, Walker was born in Massachusetts and dove into the Civil Rights Movement in 1953, shortly after receiving his PhD from Virginia Union in Richmond. He and Dr. King met as students and became friends. Not shying away from confrontation, Walker was arrested in the early 1950s after leading a group of Blacks through a whites-only door at a local library. He eventually cofounded the Congress of Racial Equality (CORE) in 1958 and conducted sit-ins at Trailways bus counters in 1960.

"The federal government was against us, the local communities were against us, the judges were against us, but we managed to do it, and I guess we found the strength to do it because it was a moral fight," Dr. Walker told the *New York Times* in 2006. He died in 2018.

During his career, Walker served as a social action model for many Black Virginians, and Harris had every intention of following in Walker's footsteps. His first move was to instigate a boycott of the local, white-owned newspaper, the *Hopewell News*, which eventually closed in 2018 after about ninety-seven years of existence. Like most southern papers, it had segregated news: one section contained white social news, the other "Colored News." As any resident knew, the only way to get into the other section of the paper was to get arrested. Just as in Montgomery, the choice of protest weapon was nonviolence.

"We recommended that everyone stop taking the paper," Harris said.

That didn't sit well with the paper's owners, who promptly sued. The case made it to court about a year later but was mired in confusion. "They forgot to subpoena us," Harris said. So, when the defendants' names were called the first day of the trial, no one was there. The judge continued the case until the next day. "We had someone alerting us to what was going on," Harris continued. Subpoenas were nailed to the front doors of the defendants' houses, but the defendants didn't go home—they gathered in a local hotel. The next day, Harris said, the newspaper's attorney "was red-faced" when no one, again, arrived in court.

Financially unable to continue a case that had already dragged on for a year, the newspaper offered to settle for $500, Harris said, ending the dispute on a paltry note. "They agreed they wouldn't mess with us no more, and we wouldn't mess with them no more," he recalled.

The paper was sold to new owners almost immediately after the settlement. Harris said he had no idea that the newspaper was struggling, or he would not have accepted the agreement. "The paper was losing money because no one (who was) Black was buying it," Harris said. Businesses that advertised to the Black community pulled their advertising, dramatically undercutting revenue. "I didn't know we were so close to closing the newspaper," Harris said.

The next move came against the city's segregated public pool. "We couldn't use it even though it was owned by the city, so we went to the council meeting and offered to buy it," Harris said. "We put up $1." The proposal was naturally rejected, but the city closed the pool rather than let Blacks and whites swim together. "They brought in dirt and filled it up," Harris said.

The city eventually did build another municipal pool as part of a recreation center. "I opposed it," Harris said, "because they got money from HUD (U.S. Department of Housing and Urban Development.) I went to HUD and held them up for some time, and HUD did all they could. Everyone's got rules and regulations on how you can do what you can do. I went as far as I could."

The city insisted anyone using the pool had to have a membership, which allowed officials to limit participation. According to Harris, the city does have a rule that any kid from a low-income family can go for free. Few Black residents actually signed up, he said, but not for racial reasons. "Black folks are not interested in the municipal swimming pool," Harris said.

There had been a small wading pool in front of Harris's high school with swings and a merry-go-round nearby. That was the recreation for the entire Black community, Harris recalled. He preferred to play sports like croquet and baseball out in the fields. Time hadn't made a swimming pool any more alluring.

Slowly evolving into a recognized leader of local Black activists, Harris now aimed at an obvious sore spot: segregated public businesses. Naturally, he chose to use sit-ins, which had become the popular protest method.

They were a technique borrowed from similar protests held by the labor movement thirty years earlier. Back then, Union organizers in the auto and steel industries got workers simply to sit by their machines, preventing both production and replacement workers from stepping in. While that approach had been used sporadically for civil rights issues from the 1930s through the 1950s, it didn't really take off as a favorite tactic until February 1, 1960, when four North Carolina Agricultural and Technical College students entered F.W. Woolworth's in Greensboro, North Carolina, and sat down at a whites-only lunch counter. Sit-ins continued there for six months.

In a National Public Radio broadcast in 2008, one of the students, Franklin McCain, explained his feelings when he took his seat on that stool.

> *Fifteen seconds after…I had the most wonderful feeling. I had a feeling of liberation, restored manhood. I had a natural high. And I truly felt almost invincible. Mind you, [I was] just sitting on a dumb stool and not having asked for service yet. It's a feeling that I don't think that I'll ever be able to have again. It's the kind of thing that people pray for…and wish for all their lives and never experience it. And I felt as though I wouldn't have been cheated out of life had that been the end of my life at that second or that moment.*

Paul M. Gaston, emeritus professor of history at the University of Virginia, described the impact of that protest.

> *This Greensboro coffee party sparked a movement that spread like brush fire across the South. In many Southern cities…young students began presenting themselves at lunch counters, making an order, and not leaving when they were asked to. They were subject to abuse; they were subject to violence; they were subject to torment. But they stayed, and the movement spread all over the region. They were young people; they were urban; they were middle class, in aspiration if not in status. And by April they had created for themselves an organization, the Student Nonviolent Coordinating Committee, which is called familiarly SNCC ("Snick"), which became the sort of shock troop movement of the young students. By September of 1961, according to a Southern Regional Council estimate, 70,000 blacks and whites had actively participated in sit-ins.*

Dr. King chimed in, describing student sit-ins as an "electrifying movement of Negro students [that] shattered the placid surface of campuses and communities across the South." He was particularly proud that the actions were "initiated, fed and sustained by students."

The first sit-in with a Virginia address occurred on February 10, 1960, when students from the all-Black Hampton Institute marched into an F.W. Woolworth store there. Students stayed without incident for three hours before leaving. Other sit-ins followed in the Hampton chain store. They attracted wide interest. In nearby Petersburg, just nine miles from Hopewell, on February 23, 1960, fifteen to twenty Black students took their seats at a S.S. Kresge Company counter. Soon after, high schoolers invaded whites-only lunch counters at McClellan's and the W.T. Grant Company.

The companies responded by closing their lunch counters, a common reaction.

At the end of the month, approximately 140 African American students from Peabody High School and Virginia State College, led by the Reverend Dr. Wyatt Tee Walker, occupied all the available seats inside the Petersburg Public Library, which required Blacks to enter through the side door and only use a designated part of the library. Additional sit-ins took place there on March 7 and 8, followed by demonstrations at Blue Bird and Century Theaters, Spiro's Department Store and the Trailways Bus Station, among other locales. In response, the city shuttered the library in July and didn't reopen it until November while approving a tougher ordinance against trespassing.

By the end of the year, the protests caused Petersburg to end segregation in all public facilities and business. Overall, students led sit-ins in twenty-three Virginia communities, including Hopewell. More than 11,000 people participated. At least 235 participants were arrested on such charges as trespassing, violation of municipal ordinances against passing out handbills, disorderly conduct and violation of city codes prohibiting public parades, demonstrations, or speeches in public places without written permission of the city manager. Several people were hurt. In Portsmouth, white teenagers injured two Black men with wrenches and hammers. Police had to use dogs to end two days of rioting there. In Petersburg, a store manager sprayed three Black high school students with ammonia.

Inspired by activities in Petersburg, Harris began to lead sit-ins. "We went to George's Drugstore—they wouldn't serve us. We went to Grant's Drugstore—they wouldn't serve us. We went to Central Drugstore—they wouldn't serve us. I saw social evils rampant in our area. We were handicapped; we couldn't participate. So, we went to jail, and we had several demonstrations and marches in the city of Hopewell. More than 75 people were arrested."

The arrests occurred when Harris marched into one of the three George's Rexall Drugstores in Hopewell with a contingent of men and women for a sit-in. Harris's son Kenneth recalled the brief confrontation at George's. In Hopewell, and probably many other southern cities, store policy was to allow Blacks to buy something to eat or drink but not consume it inside. Protestors intended to change that. Kenneth said that the idea of marching and doing sit-ins didn't appeal to him. He had been part of one previously at a Woolworth's.

"You could go in and buy anything you want," he said, "but you couldn't sit at the lunch counter. I was a little guy then, and I could see underneath the lunch counter. There was chewing gum from one end of the lunch counter another. I never saw anything so filthy in my life. I said, 'I don't want to come down here anyway. It's filthy. Why would I want to sit here?'"

His father focused not on the dirt but on a more important issue.

There was a brief scuffle at George's. One of the protestors, identified only as Leroy, apparently hadn't attended the nonviolent training class, Harris noted, with tongue in cheek. He wasn't totally kidding: there were classes conducted by activists from the SCLC. When the police arrived in George's, Harris and a handful of his companions were arrested under a 1934 Virginia trespassing law, which had been upgraded in 1960, probably in response to the sit-ins mushrooming nationally. New penalties increased the fine to $1,000 or up to twelve months in jail.

"I was doing what we were supposed to do: sit down there and wait until the policeman came," Kenneth said. "Then the police arrested all of us and marched us across the street to the jail." He was twelve or thirteen years old. "I had never been behind bars before," he said.

Kenneth didn't remember what happened in court, but the experience affected him several years later. He went to get a driver's license, which, because of his previous arrest, required approval from a judge. "I can remember him looking at me. He asked me if I'm going to do this anymore. I said, 'No.' If I had said yes, I wouldn't have been able to get my license."

Kenneth's father wasn't willing to concede so easily. His case—Hopewell's last sit-in and trespassing trial—ended up in the United States District Court in Virginia, which continued to advocate for racial segregation. The justices ruled against Harris in March 1961 that "no proof appears of discrimination against Negroes in the invocation of the statutes. There are no instances adduced of differentiation between the races in the execution of these laws. Indeed, the evidence reveals that both whites and Negroes were arrested for the transgressions, as well as persons identified as 'Moorish Americans,' who are described as being neither white nor Negro." The court also took a swing at the U.S. Supreme Court, demanding that federal courts stop interfering in the activities of state courts.

It was a futile gesture. Businesses couldn't endure the subsequent losses. By the end of 1961, Woolworth's and other chain stores had desegregated their lunch counters nationally. However, not all store owners gave in. They waited until the Civil Rights Act of 1964, which banned racial segregation "by businesses offering food, lodging, gasoline, or entertainment to the public."

That same year, Harris's case reached the Supreme Court. It was bundled with similar suits under the name of *Bell v. Maryland*. Justice William J. Brennan Jr., considered the most liberal member of the court, produced the majority opinion overturning the convictions. He wrote, "When one citizen, because of his race, creed, or color, is denied the privilege of being treated as any other citizen in places of public accommodation, we have classes of citizenship, one being more degrading than the other. That is at war with the one class of citizenship created by the Thirteenth, Fourteenth, and Fifteenth Amendments."

Brennan added, "Segregation of Negroes in the restaurants and lunch counters of parts of America is a relic of slavery. It is a badge of second-class citizenship. It is a denial of a privilege and immunity of national citizenship and of the equal protection guaranteed by the Fourteenth Amendment against abridgment by the States. When the state police, the state prosecutor, and the state courts unite to convict Negroes for renouncing that relic of slavery, the 'State' violates the Fourteenth Amendment."

By then, Harris had served sixty days in jail. Released and undeterred, he joined other sit-ins in Danville, Richmond and Petersburg, getting arrested a few more times in the process. "I was home with the children during that time to take them to their games or whatever activities they were in," Ruth Harris recalled. "You know I had to be there for them and, of course, getting a bondsman to get him out of jail."

There would be more jails to come. "Dr. King inspired us to go forward," Harris said. The two men had not formally met then, but Harris had heard King speak. "I saw Dr. King in the 1950s, right after he had conducted the March bus rally in Alabama. He was invited to speak in Petersburg at the Mt. Olivette Baptist Church. And I went to the rally," Harris said. "I thought that this was ordered from God to have a man such as this to speak to us. After that, I thought it was good for me to follow him."

King actually made seven visits to Petersburg, which is located southeast of Hopewell and south of Richmond and, later, was the first Virginia

Dr. Martin Luther King Jr. (*left*) joins with the Rev Curtis W. Harris Sr. (*center*) and Milton Reid of Petersburg on July 3, 1965. *Used with permission from the* Richmond Times-Dispatch.

community to designate a day honoring the slain civil rights leader. During his stops, King recruited residents to join his staff, spoke at local Black churches, stayed overnight in the homes of local civil rights activists and addressed students at Virginia State College. Harris heard him address the twenty-first Annual Convention of the Virginia State NAACP in a church in 1956. There, King spoke to an enormous crowd. The number of people who wanted to hear him exceeded the church's capacity, so the speech was broadcast to other churches.

"We were not used to those kinds of crowds," recalled the Reverend Wyatt Tee Walker, then pastor of the Gillfield Baptist Church, the second-oldest black Baptist church in Virginia and one of the oldest in the nation.

Organized in 1797 in Petersburg as an integrated congregation, the church moved to its present site on Perry Street in 1818. The area was named for Revolutionary veteran Erasmus Gill and is not to be confused with Gilfield Baptist in Ivor, where Harris was pastor. Petersburg and Ivor are about thirty-eight miles apart.

In 1961, Harris and King finally shook hands.

That year, Harris achieved statewide recognition of a sort. After the epochal 1954 Supreme Court decision *Brown v. Topeka Board of Education*, Virginia's Democrat senator Harry Byrd Jr. launched a campaign called Massive Resistance in an effort to counter the law. He announced in 1956 that "if we can organize the Southern States for massive resistance to this order, I think that in time the rest of the country will realize that racial integration is not going to be accepted in the South."

Byrd managed to get the Virginia state legislature to approve a variety of laws designed to hold onto the old system. One law prohibited integrated schools from getting state funding; another allowed the governor to shut down any school. In addition, the state set up tuition grants so students could attend private institutions, a concept still floated around the country under the guise of "vouchers." The NAACP stepped in with a series of lawsuits

Rev. Curtis W. Harris Sr. (*third from left*) meets with Dr. Martin Luther King Jr. (*second from left*) and other civil rights leaders in Richmond, Virginia. *Used with permission from the Valentine Corporation.*

that eventually overturned the legislation. Federal troops were never needed to enforce the laws, but Governor J. Lindsay Almond did shut some Virginia school systems for as long as a year. The battle would continue until 1986, with court-ordered busing mandated by the courts in selected communities.

Harris ran afoul of the new laws that evolved from the Massive Resistance movement. The legislative committee of the Virginia General Assembly cited him for contempt for failing to disclose names of other members of his organization or respond to questions asked him by one of two Virginia committees created to enforce racial laws. One group was titled the Committee on Law Reform and Racial Activities, known as the Thomson Commission for its chairman, Jim Thomson of Alexandria, a brother-in-law of Senator Byrd. The other one, which Harris also faced, was the Committee on Offenses Against the Administration of Justice, better known as the Boatwright Commission for its chairman, John B. Boatwright Sr., an attorney from Buckingham. The two groups later merged. Boatwright, who served in the state legislature for thirty-eight years and died in 1965, also was a leader of Massive Resistance.

The Boatwright Commission developed seven laws in support of segregation and against the NAACP and other organizations. In 1956, those laws were passed by the Virginia General Assembly.

The NAACP filed suit against the Boatwright Commission in 1958, arguing that the commission members "are acting as part of a conspiracy engaged in by the elected officials of Virginia to intimidate, discourage and impede the plaintiffs and all Negro citizens of Virginia from using the courts as a means of ending the practices of racial segregation in that state." The suit also claimed that the legislature "created the defendant committee for the sole purpose of harassing and intimidating the plaintiffs in their efforts as lawyers to serve the cause of desegregation."

Harris agreed with that assessment. "The Boatwright Commission was a legislative committee set up by the legislature in Virginia, and their aim was to put fear in the minds and the hearts of African-Americans. It is no different than the Ku Klux Klan, just more sophisticated," Harris said. The committee "picked on people who were known activists. All of us who were in that category were subpoenaed by the committee. Some of us decided that we were not going to cooperate with segregation."

Harris said the committee was looking for information that could be used to identify participants. "They were trying to harass African American people who came to our mass meetings," Harris continued. "Eventually, they would not come back because the police would be on their case. We assumed that that was what was going to happen. We were not going to support segregation, even when the law was trying to harass us."

Refusal to talk carried consequences. "The legislature then charged us in Circuit-Court in Hopewell," Harris recalled. The defendants were ordered "to come before the court to determine whether or not we should go to jail because we wouldn't answer the question of a legislative committee. I went two or three times before the circuit court."

He did not go alone. During the trial on March 29, 1962, dozens of ministers from Virginia and other prominent Black leaders, including King, joined the process to serve as silent witnesses to the event. All who attended dressed in black clergy robes.

Harris said that when the judge stepped into the courtroom, codefendant

A *Tri-City News* account of Dr. Martin Luther King *(center)* and the Reverend Milton Reid *(right)* supporting Rev. Curtis W. Harris Sr. at his 1962 trial for refusing to supply information to a Virginia state committee. *Courtesy of Swem Library, College of William & Mary.*

Dr. Milton Reid stood up and asked everyone to pray. "He stopped the judge dead in his tracks, and he also bowed his head," Harris said. After taking his seat on the bench, the judge then ordered no more such demonstrations in the courtroom. Reid, who died in 2010, recalled walking with other Black children to school in segregationist Norfolk County while white students used school buses. When they rode by, white children sometimes spit and yelled at Reid and his friends, he said. The insults inspired Reid to battle against racial injustice.

Reid had plenty of opportunities to demonstrate his spunk elsewhere. In the early 1960s, he forced Petersburg Hospital to stop segregating patients and was arrested for eating in the whites-only area of a Petersburg bus terminal cafe. He founded the Virginia Chapter of the SCLC, which counted Harris among its members, and served on the state advisory committee of the U.S. Civil Rights Commission.

The case against Reed, Harris and the others proceeded slowly. "I went to court two or three times regarding that case," Harris said. "Finally, the judge decided that he was going to drop the case—throw it out of court. He warned me that the next time that I went before the Committee that I had to answer all legitimate questions."

Harris did it in his own way. "They wanted to know my name, my address and who were with me in the organization, and what was the name of the organization. I didn't answer any questions. I took the Fifth Amendment on all of the questions, including my name," he explained.

The commission also made an end run, sending officers to the Black law firm of Jordon, Dawley and Holt, who were advising Black activists like Harris, looking for records and correspondence relating to the U.S. Congress of Racial Equality, SCLC, Virginia Christian Leadership Conference and other Black improvement associations in the state's larger cities. The approach worked. Lawyers found themselves in court, defending their reputations and facing disbarment. NAACP membership promptly dropped by 33 percent. Famed Black activist attorney Oliver Hill told the media that was because of "intimidation, harassment and economic reprisals" against anyone identified as supporting Black causes. Hill knew something about that. In 1955, KKK members burned a cross on his front lawn.

The harassment did not end until a 1963 Supreme Court decision, *NAACP v. Burton*, absolved NAACP attorneys. "A state may not, under the guise of prohibiting professional misconduct, ignore constitutional rights," Justice Brennan wrote in the 6–3 decision.

Inspired, Harris kept busy. "We had sit-ins, lay-ins, and swim-ins, and we even filed a suit to integrate the local cemetery," he said.

"I don't recall seeing him afraid of anything," said his son, Michael, who now lives in Maryland.

Then, in 1966, Harris learned that Hopewell officials planned to build a landfill in the African American community. "They called it a landfill; I called it a dump," Harris said. "We did a lot of work on that, and it turned out that they are going to build it anyway. They tried to find a way to get it without going through the African-American community, but it would cost them too much, so they decided they are going to go on through the African-American community."

To attract attention about the landfill, Harris organized a march. "We were going to start the march at the dump and go from the dump down to city hall. I guess it is about two and a half miles, maybe three miles. Our folk didn't show up, except a few. I looked but didn't have but about 14 people."

Harris decided to stall. The police were on overtime. City officials wanted to know if there was going to be a march. If not, they could cut costs and send the police home. Meanwhile, Harris continued waiting for more of his followers to show up.

"Somebody in a cab came down to the entrance to the dump, and he was very, very excited," Harris recalled. "He said, 'Don't go downtown. The Ku Klux Klan is downtown, waiting for you.'"

Federal reports at the time indicate that the KKK only had about two thousand members in the whole state because of government pressure against the hate group. An estimated twenty-two of them were marching down the street toward city hall in the opposite direction from Harris's position.

Harris replied, "I said that I didn't want to disappoint the Ku Klux Klan. I had to go downtown. That's when we started to march. We only had 14 people. I didn't march on sidewalks. If I had to walk on the sidewalk, there wasn't going to be no march. I said I'm going to walk in the street. So, I marched, and all the people that we were passing by, we were beckoning them to join the march. By the time we got downtown, we had 45 people in the march. The Ku Klux Klan was waiting for us at city hall. There were about 35 or 40 of them. And they had on the robes and even had some children with robes on, too."

A photo taken that day shows Harris in front of a small band of protestors, striding forward with a determined gait. He is carrying a petition in opposition to the proposed dump. There are three men and one child behind him, along with two uniformed policemen. Men and women in white robes, faces uncovered as a result of a state law banning masks, line both sides of the city hall stairs. More white people are casually standing on the sidewalk on both sides of the Klan.

According to newspaper accounts, the marchers chanted, "Freedom, Freedom now." Klansmen answered, "Never, never."

One member of the Klan told the local newspaper that the group's policy was "never, never accept integration; never submit to Communism." He didn't explain how those two ideas were related.

"When the police saw us coming, they spread the Ku Klux Klan on both sides of the walkway so that we could go through in front of them," Harris said. "So, we went to the city hall and stood on the steps. The Ku Klux Klan was flanked on both sides. We went into the city hall, and the (acting) city manager was waiting for us, and I delivered the paper to him. He had the door locked into city hall, so nobody could get in. So, they let me in, and a couple people with me, and they allowed me to serve that paper on the city manager."

Harris and his colleagues then went back outside. "We started to sing some civil rights songs. The Ku Klux Klan drowned us out, chanting 'Never, never, never…' We then turned around and started to kneel on the steps with our back to the Ku Klux Klan, and I said I wanted to pray. One of the Ku Klux Klan said that every man ought to have a chance to pray, and they shut up.

"I had a long prayer," Harris continued. According to media reports, he called for "human justice here in the presence of those who hate us." Harris said, "After I got through praying, the Ku Klux Klan preacher started to pray. When he got through praying, we turned around and stood up, and they filed away one by one. They never said any more words. We were interested in marching, showing off, so we marched from city hall, figuring that we had won a victory and marched all the way back to the church. The police stopping the traffic for us, but the Ku Klux Klan never showed up again."

By the time Harris faced off against the hooded members of the KKK, he was already a member of the board of the national SCLC. His defining moment did not come in Hopewell, although the various protests there helped give Harris a national platform and propelled him even farther into the top levels of the Civil Rights Movement. His opportunity came in 1964, marching side by side with Dr. King as part of the most significant event of the Civil Rights Movement.

CHAPTER 6

NATIONAL INVOLVEMENT

DANVILLE, BIRMINGHAM, SELMA
AND WASHINGTON, D.C.

B y 1963, Harris was no longer confining his attention to tiny Hopewell. As civil rights protests radiated around the region, he found himself drawn to participate. That year, for example, he joined activists in Danville, which is located southeast of Richmond on the border with North Carolina.

Danville, known for textile manufacturing, was about 25 percent African American in 1960. Its median income trailed the rest of the state, adding to dissention. Ironically, Danville had been one of the more enlightened racial communities in the state. In the late 1800s, Black residents constituted about 60 percent of the population. In 1883, voters elected a group of African Americans, moderate whites and Republicans to head the city under the name "Readjusters."

However, in response, when fall elections rolled around, segregationists initiated a riot that left four Black residents dead and four wounded. Blacks promptly resigned from city council and the police force as racial intolerance took hold for the next nearly eighty years. Occasional lawsuits and demands for equality led nowhere until 1960, when sixteen Black high school students walked into the all-white Danville Memorial Library. The city promptly closed the library. It reopened in September following a federal court ruling.

For a year, leaders of the local NAACP and SCLC chapters went before the Danville City Council to call for desegregation of city boards. In 1962, they filed suit in federal court, calling for integration of the city's hospitals, schools, cemeteries, public buildings, public housing projects and teaching assignments. In response, Black leaders were arrested at a segregated Howard Johnson restaurant for trespassing.

Unhappy with progress, activists created the Danville Christian Progressive Association (DCPA) and affiliated with the Southern Christian Leadership Council, the organization Harris had joined.

Buoyed by the Birmingham protests in 1963, DCPA began to act. First, in June, members marched into city hall and occupied the city manager's office. A day later, two hundred people demonstrated in front of the Danville Municipal Building. Danville Corporation Court judge Archibald Aiken responded with a temporary injunction, ordering protestors to stop "among other things, assembling in an unlawful manner, interfering with traffic and business, obstructing entrances to businesses and public buildings, participating and inciting mob violence, and using loud language that disrupts the peace," according to civil rights files in the Library of Virginia.

That didn't work. Newspaper accounts report that "on June 10, sixty high school students marched to the municipal building. The leaders were arrested. The others fled and were chased into a blind alley where high-pressure hoses were turned on them. Many were knocked down and some had their clothes blown off. Using nightsticks on helpless students, police officers arrested them and hauled them off to jail." That same day, DCPA set up a prayer meeting but were attacked by police and deputized garbagemen; forty-seven were injured.

Aiken then called a special grand jury, which indicted three demonstration leaders on charges of "conspiring to incite the colored population of the State to acts of violence and war against the white population." He relied on an 1859 statute enacted after John Brown's failed raid on Harper's Ferry, Virginia, in 1859. Soon after, the grand jury used the Brown statute to indict ten more protestors. By August, an estimated three hundred people were awaiting trial. Bail was set high, straining finances, while some trials were moved miles away, further agonizing defendants.

That only fueled more demonstrations, with national and state leaders, including Harris, arriving to add their support. Dr. King gave a speech in July. Still, by mid-July, more than "250 people had been arrested on charges of contempt, trespassing, disorderly conduct, assault, parading without a permit, and resisting arrest. Parents were arrested when they went to the jail to post bail for their children for contributing to the delinquency of a minor by not providing adequate supervision," according to the Library of Virginia's "Guide to the 1963 Danville (Va.) Civil Rights Case Files, 1963–

1973." An estimated 600 people, including Harris, were eventually taken to jail. Harris was charged with inciting to riot.

The U.S. Supreme Court eventually voted 5–4 to uphold the legality of the injunction. Judge Archibald Aiken, national known for his anti-desegregation views, started hearing the cases locally in 1966, some three years after the protests. The worst penalty was 250 days in jail and a $2,500 fine for a local leader. However, most of the convictions were thrown out of court in 1973. Eventually, Danville collected only about $5,000 in fines. Meanwhile, the SCLC was able to negotiate with city officials to integrate the city police force.

The Danville protests were overshadowed by events further south in Birmingham, Alabama, then considered the most racist city in the country. King certainly agreed with that assessment and said so in writing. Birmingham was a center of KKK activities. The Klan did not hesitate to strike. Members castrated an African American in one horrible episode. Not content with such violence, they had gone far beyond ridiculous by trying to get a book banned because it contained pictures of both black and white rabbits. They also wanted music produced by Black musicians cut from radio programs.

The city was completely divided on racial grounds, all legally ascribed by rigid laws. As a consequence, only 10 percent of the Black population was registered to vote. Black residents couldn't be employed in a variety of jobs, including those in police and fire departments. They couldn't be hired as salesclerks, bus drivers, bank tellers or store cashiers. Black secretaries couldn't even work for white professionals. Naturally, the effect was economic: Blacks earned half the average annual income of whites, and unemployment was 2.5 times worse in the Black community.

The commissioner of public safety, Eugene "Bull" Connor, was unknown nationally, but Birmingham residents knew him as a virulent racist. An estimated fifty racially motivated bombings had taken place in the city between 1945 and 1962. None had been solved. Connor blamed the bombings of Black churches on "Negroes." He threatened bloodshed if desegregation efforts continued. His hatred was so palpable that he actually inspired sympathy for Black protestors. President John Kennedy noted that the "Civil Rights Movement should thank God for Bull Connor. He helped it as much as Abraham Lincoln."

Black residents had tried to fight back. For example, the NAACP was banned in Alabama in 1956—the state said the organization violated a state law requiring out-of-state corporations to register. The ban was finally overturned by the U.S. Supreme Court in 1964 when the newly formed Alabama Christian Movement for Civil Rights (ACMCR) sued the city to open its public parks. After losing in court, Birmingham simply closed the parks anyway. ACMCR's founder, the Reverend Fred Shuttlesworth, was arrested and jailed in 1962. His house and church were bombed. After his letter to the mayor was openly discarded, Shuttlesworth petitioned King and the SCLC for help.

"If you come to Birmingham," he wrote, "you will not only gain prestige, but really shake the country. If you win in Birmingham, as Birmingham goes, so goes the nation."

Shuttlesworth's role has been largely forgotten amid the ensuing events, despite his prominence then. "Without Fred Shuttlesworth laying the groundwork, those demonstrations in Birmingham would not have been as successful," Andrew M. Manis, author of Shuttlesworth's biography *A Fire You Can't Put Out*, told the *New York Times* when Shuttlesworth died in 2011. "Birmingham led to Selma, and those two became the basis of the civil rights struggle. Shuttlesworth," Manis added, had "no equal in terms of courage and putting his life in the line of fire" to battle segregation.

Prior to the Birmingham march, Shuttlesworth was arrested between thirty and forty times for holding peaceful marches, spent time in jail and somehow survived bombings. In one instance, in 1956, someone set off dynamite outside his bedroom. The mattress saved his life. A year later, while trying to enroll his children in a white school, Shuttlesworth was attacked by Klansmen armed with bicycle chains and brass knuckles. When a doctor treating Shuttlesworth's injuries marveled that he had not suffered a concussion, Shuttlesworth famously replied, "Doctor, the Lord knew I lived in a hard town, so he gave me a hard head."

King accepted the challenge to come to Birmingham after failing to succeed in Albany, Georgia, the year before. In Birmingham, the SCLC honed its tactics to focus on desegregating the downtown shopping and government district. If successful, its demands would then expand to include fair hiring practices as well as desegregation of the city's schools.

"We wanted confrontation, nonviolent confrontation, to see if it would work," Shuttlesworth said. "Not just for Birmingham—for the nation. We were trying to launch a systematic, wholehearted battle against segregation, which would set the pace for the nation."

Protests built on student efforts begun the year before. Activists set up boycotts of downtown businesses, cutting sales up to 40 percent. The city responded by slicing money from a surplus food program that targeted poor Black families. An intense spring boycott increased the pressure. Some businesses succumbed and removed "whites only" signs. Connor promptly threatened to take away business licenses if the owners didn't obey segregation laws.

The next step was to confront the racist forces head on, just as Harris did in Hopewell. Wyatt Tee Walker, then executive director of the SCLC, was very direct about the approach. "My theory was that if we mounted a strong nonviolent movement, the opposition would surely do something to attract the media, and in turn induce national sympathy and attention to the everyday segregated circumstance of a person living in the Deep South," he said.

Connor was only too happy to oblige. He sicced police dogs on the protesters and turned fire houses on them, drawing national attention. Shuttlesworth suffered chest injuries when he was hit by a blast of water. Years later, he would be honored by President Barack Obama, and his name was attached to the local Birmingham airport.

In Birmingham. King was arrested for defying an injunction that denied his right to march. Kept in solitary confinement and refused the right to see his lawyer, he wrote now-famed letters from the jail that gained further attention and support. In them, he said:

> One who breaks an unjust law must do so openly, lovingly, and with a willingness to accept the penalty. I submit that an individual who breaks a law that conscience tells him is unjust and who willingly accepts the penalty of imprisonment in order to arouse the conscience of the community over its injustice, is in reality expressing the highest respect for law.

Only President Kennedy's intervention got King released. However, the home belonging to King's brother was bombed, along with the motel room where King stayed.

Children were encouraged to join the anti-segregation march. Video of the youngsters being attacked by Connor's dogs and sprayed with water from high-pressure hoses filled television sets nationwide and helped shift public attitudes in favor of civil rights for African Americans. Eventually, 1,100 students who had attended the demonstrations were expelled for truancy from city schools and colleges. A federal court order was needed to get them reinstated.

The events in Birmingham resounded nationally. During a ten-week period that spring, an estimated 758 demonstrations in 186 cities led to 14,733 arrests. In June, President Kennedy responded by calling civil rights "a moral issue" and announcing a push for federal civil rights legislation.

The events were capped by the famed March on Washington for Jobs and Freedom that had been initiated by A. Philip Randolph, international president of the Brotherhood of Sleeping Car Porters, president of the Negro American Labor Council and vice president of the AFL-CIO. In addition, five of the largest civil rights organizations in the United States signed on as sponsors. Despite private misgivings, Kennedy also announced his support for the march in an effort to gain support for his civil rights bill.

Harris and his sons Curtis Jr. and Kenneth were among the estimated 250,000 people who swarmed into the nation's capital, spreading across the National Mall from the steps of the Lincoln Memorial. At that time, the marchers represented the largest gathering of protesters in the Capitol's history. At eleven o'clock in the morning on August 28, they met by the Washington Monument and marched the mile to the Lincoln Memorial.

Black leaders met with a bipartisan congressional delegation and exited the Capitol around noon. John Lewis—at that time head of the Student Nonviolent Coordinating Committee (SNCC), before being elected to Congress—was shocked by the size of the crowd. He saw "a sea of humanity coming from Union Station. We got out of our cars. We were supposed to be leading the march, but the people were already marching."

As the day's final speaker, King delivered the "I Have a Dream" speech that still resonates around this country. The program ended at 4:20 in the afternoon, ten minutes ahead of schedule.

Andrew Young, a King aide who eventually served as mayor of Atlanta and a UN ambassador, said everyone was elated. "You have to remember I was 31," he said. "Martin Luther King was 33 or 34, and we were young. We were like kids that had just won a football game, smiling and cracking jokes…"

However, in much of the South, the response was anything but positive. First, on September 16, less than a month after the march on Washington, a bomb exploded at the Sixteenth Street Baptist Church, killing four young girls. The church, today designated as a national landmark, had been the first Black church in Birmingham and a center of local Black activism. Major speakers, like singer Paul Robeson, educator Mary McLeod Bethune and activist W.E. B. DuBois, had graced its pulpit. In the 1960s, the church functioned as the headquarters of local Black leaders and the site of mass meetings.

Despite the bloodshed, the drive to end racial discrimination continued unabated. Passage of the 1964 Civil Rights Act was spurred by the bombing and resultant outcry. Kennedy introduced it by openly stating the facts of Black life in the 1960s:

The Negro baby born in America today, regardless of the section of the nation in which he is born, has about one-half as much chance of completing high school as a white baby born in the same place on the same day; one third as much chance of completing college; one third as much chance of becoming a professional man; twice as much chance of becoming unemployed; about one-seventh as much chance of earning $10,000 a year; a life expectancy which is seven years shorter; and the prospects of earning only half as much.

Overcoming an initial filibuster by southern Democrats, the bill became law almost exactly one year later. It ended racial discrimination in public places, such as theaters, restaurants and hotels. At the same time, the law required equal employment opportunities. In addition, turning presidential directives into federal law, organizations receiving money from the government could be cut off with the discovery of discrimination based on color, race or national origin. The law, passed and signed by President Lyndon Johnson less than a year after Kennedy's assassination, undercut state laws that restricted voting and gave the U.S. attorney general the power to step in when violations were discovered.

Although there was widespread approval of the sweeping legislation, complete civil rights remained a dream. In 1965, Harris joined with King and other Black leaders in what became the pivotal event in the entire decade: the fifty-four-mile march from Selma to Montgomery for voting rights. Years later, when the march was commemorated, then-senator Barack Obama pushed an ailing Rev. Shuttlesworth in a wheelchair along the route.

The SNCC and the SCLC had been campaigning together for voting rights. An estimated 2 percent of the fifteen thousand Black residents in Montgomery were registered to vote; the rest had been stymied by poll taxes, literacy tests and other restrictions. The efforts focused on Selma and nearby Marion, twenty-five miles northwest of Selma, until February 18, when an Alabama state trooper in Marion shot Jimmie Lee Jackson, a twenty-six-year-old church deacon who had fled into a café in an ill-fated attempt to protect his mother from the trooper's nightstick.

Jackson died on February 26. His death prompted leaders to call for a march to Montgomery "with Jimmie Jackson, [to] take his body and lay it on the steps of the capital," according to a Marion civil rights organizer. The decision to take the protest directly to the state capital drew widespread interest, despite Governor George Wallace of Alabama's vow to prevent it.

Rev. Curtis W. Harris Sr. (*left*) was in the forefront of the historic Selma march in March 1966. *Courtesy of Andrew Shannon.*

Rev. Curtis W. Harris participating in the historic Selma march in 1966. *Courtesy of Andrew Shannon.*

"There never was a moment in American history more honorable and more inspiring than the pilgrimage of clergymen and laymen of every race and faith pouring into Selma to face danger at the side of its embattled Negroes," King said in a speech before they set out.

On Sunday, March 7, 1965, about six hundred civil rights marchers left Selma and walked east on U.S. 80. At the Edmund Pettus Bridge— named for a Confederate officer, a former Grand Dragon of the KKK and a U.S. senator—about six blocks from the starting point, they were assaulted by about two hundred local and state police. They were hit with clubs and tear gas, forcing them back to Selma. The day became known as Bloody Sunday. The attack was not unexpected. As in Birmingham, Black leaders knew local sheriff Jim Clark was likely to react violently and hoped the resulting mayhem, televised nationally, would draw more support to their side.

They were right: the unprovoked attack on peaceful marchers appalled viewers. Dripping blood from a head wound, SNCC leader John Lewis said, "I don't see how President Johnson can send troops to Vietnam—I don't see how he can send troops to the Congo—I don't see how he can send troops to Africa and can't send troops to Selma."

King, who won the Nobel Peace Prize in October that year, took advantage of a brief lull to call on "religious leaders from all over the nation to join us on Tuesday in our peaceful, nonviolent march for freedom." Harris answered the telegram sent to him and headed south.

Two days later, King led the marchers to the bridge again while seeking court protection. Once there, they knelt and prayed in front of state troopers who blocked the road. Then, the marchers turned around.

Meanwhile, Federal District Court judge Frank M. Johnson Jr. issued a ruling allowing the march to proceed peacefully. "The law is clear that the right to petition one's government for the redress of grievances may be exercised in large groups…and these rights may be exercised by marching, even along public highways," he wrote.

Appointed by President Dwight Eisenhower, Johnson was the same judge who had ruled a decade earlier against the Montgomery bus company's effort to maintain segregated buses. To the anger of former college classmate George Wallace, then governor of Alabama, Johnson also demanded that the names of qualified African Americans be added to county voting rolls. In addition, he wrote the first statewide school desegregation decree. In return, his mother's house was bombed. A cross was burned on his lawn. Police were often called in to protect his home and family.

Some thirty years after Johnson's decision allowed the marchers to proceed, President Bill Clinton awarded him the Presidential Medal of Freedom, the nation's highest civilian award. The citation read: "His landmark decisions in the areas of desegregation, voting rights and civil liberties transformed our understanding of the Constitution."

With Judge Johnson's order in hand, King prepared the march. Johnson's directive limited them to three hundred marchers along a two-lane highway. They would be protected by the Alabama National Guard—which had been federalized by an order from President Johnson—and FBI agents. Meanwhile, President Johnson submitted the Voting Rights Act to Congress.

Exactly two weeks after Bloody Sunday, the marchers set out for Montgomery, walking twelve to seventeen miles a day and sleeping in supporter's yards along the way. Harris, forty-one, was with them during those four hot, humid days. Entertainers like Harry Belafonte and Lena Horne put on impromptu concerts.

"It was difficult," Harris said. "I remember one leg of the march, when we came through an area that the police could not guard us through. We had police around us, and there was a helicopter over our heads, but we were afraid that somebody was going to shoot Dr. King. So, we made ourselves barriers around him until we got through that area. I was expecting a bullet any minute, but we got through it. It was very, very scary." Six men, including Harris, locked arms to serve as a human shield around King.

Harris had a right to be afraid. The evening before the marchers set out, a white Unitarian minister named James Reeb was attacked by a group of white thugs and killed. That forced President Johnson to contact Governor Wallace and demand he protect the marchers. Wallace refused.

As the marchers continued, people began to join them, including two assistant U.S. attorney generals. By the time they arrived at the capital on

Thursday, March 25, an estimated twenty-five thousand people had swelled their ranks. Once inside Montgomery, they sang:

Keep your eyes on the prize, hold on, hold on.
I've never been to heaven, but I think I'm right,
You won't find George Wallace anywhere in sight.

King stood on the Montgomery capital steps in a final rally and said, "The end we seek is a society at peace with itself, a society that can live with its conscience. And that will be a day not of the white man, not of the Black man. That will be the day of man as man."

Wallace was not impressed and declined to take a petition calling for voting rights. The peaceful march then ended on a violent note when, that night, a housewife from Michigan who was helping transport the marchers home to Selma was shot and killed by Klansmen.

Nevertheless, on August 6, less than six months later, President Johnson signed the Voting Rights Act of 1965 into law. King and several other Black leaders were in attendance. In his comments, Johnson referred to "the outrage of Selma" and called the right to vote "the most powerful instrument ever devised by man for breaking down injustice and destroying the terrible walls which imprison men because they are different from other men."

The legislation banned poll taxes and provided for the appointment of federal examiners to register qualified citizens. In many ways, the law expunged the Virginia law in which examiners had been used to prevent voting. As a direct result of the new law, in 1966, the Supreme Court held Virginia's poll tax to be unconstitutional.

Hopewell was affected by all these changes. Harris was in the middle of them, too, finally getting elected to office.

CHAPTER 7

POLITICAL

ELECTION, FIRST AFRICAN AMERICAN MAYOR, ETHANOL

Throughout the 1960s, Harris remained busy. Well known now both locally as vice president of the SCLC and statewide for his leadership in various protests, he was often asked to participate in social action. In 1969, he marched in Suffolk, Virginia, to protest discrimination in employment at a hospital there. As a result, he was beaten, arrested and sent to jail. "No one went to jail but me," Harris said.

He was getting used to that. Overall, he would be arrested and jailed thirteen times. Former state senator Henry L. Marsh III, a civil rights attorney, said Harris would come to him following an arrest. "I would tell him, 'You know, Curtis, you could go to jail,'" Marsh recalled. "He would look at me and say, 'Well what do you think I want to do?'" Marsh was the first African American mayor of Richmond and faced off against Harris politically in a race for the state senate. Marsh won and served twenty-two years before retiring in 2014.

Marsh knew Harris well. "Curtis Harris was one of the most militant civil rights activists in the history of Virginia," Marsh said. "He never saw a demonstration he didn't like. He went to Danville and participated in the Danville demonstrations. He marched with Martin Luther King Jr. from Selma to Montgomery, and he was a real fighter. He has been to the General Assembly and created a commotion up in the gallery, and they had to send me up to talk him into coming down."

Harris's militancy led to a lot of lawsuits. "We defended Curtis before everybody," Marsh continued. "I guess he got it from his days when he marched with Dr. King, but Curtis was looking for ways of demonstrating. He didn't like racial segregation and racial oppression, and he led people into pickets. Even in later years, he would go to Fort Lee to confront the general and bring the cases to me after he started one. He was one of the most active persons in dismantling segregation in Virginia that we've ever had. I was his lawyer for many of those cases."

Harris felt he had more than the law on his side. "I believe that the Lord will take care of it, but I want to help the Lord," he said. "That's why I went to jail and got beaten, got bit by dogs and so forth. I was trying to help the Lord. The Lord didn't need me, but I was trying to help."

Harris also had to perform sad chores. With his wife, he was among an array of Virginia civil rights activists at the 1968 funeral of Dr. Martin Luther King Jr., who was killed by an assassin while in Memphis, Tennessee.

In the early 1970s, however, Harris decided to retire from his activist lifestyle. He was in his fifties. Despite his best intentions, however, his reputation guaranteed he'd still be on the front lines. He recalled one day, sitting in the house, when some visitors showed up. "There was a strike at one of the plants," Harris said, "and they wanted to have a march." The unidentified chief of police had rejected that idea, and the Black and white employees were ready to take him on.

"If we can't get a march," they told Harris, "we're going to tear this town down."

Harris, however, had an appointment in Richmond the day of the planned march. He changed his schedule. Then, he called the chief. "I said that I want to start downtown and go through the community. The chief said, 'Okay.' He even promised to send someone to work out the details and did," Harris recalled.

Soon after, Harris led about five hundred marchers through Hopewell. "We took up the whole street," he said. "I don't want to walk on no sidewalk. A demonstration is to take the street." With that, his brief retirement ended.

Harris noted that the police acted professionally, reflecting a shift in the community Harris had called home since 1928. Hopewell had become more racially accommodating, starting with the schools. For starters, Patrick Copeland Elementary School was integrated in 1963, nine years after the famed *Brown v. Topeka Board of Education* ruling and four years after schools in nearby Petersburg welcomed Black students. Ironically, Copeland—named for a seventeenth-century chaplain who sailed to Virginia on the *Royal James*—had originally been planned to provide free education for indentured servants, a handful of whom were Black. The two-story brick school that

Harris knew opened in 1939. It was torn down amid controversy in 2006—some residents wanted to maintain it as an historical landmark, but the city decided not to.

In 1963, Reuben L. and Joy T. Gilliam, the Black descendants of indentured servants who once owned slaves themselves, forced desegregation of public schools by filing suit in federal court on behalf of their children, Renee Patrice and Reuben Jr. "I knew I was going to Patrick Copeland in September 1963. It was under a court order," Renee Patrice told Dr. Lauranett L. Lee, who wrote a history of African American life in Hopewell. Patrice's grandmother didn't believe it. "She didn't think she'd ever live to see Black children go to a white school," Renee Patrice said.

When the day came, Renee Patrice's grandmother rented a cab to go to the school and stood across the street in the doorway of the Appomattox Cleaners with an umbrella "to keep the morning sun off her because she wanted to see us walk into Patrick Copeland," Renee Patrice said.

High school integration quickly followed. Harris's two eldest sons, Curtis Jr. and Kenneth, attempted to enroll in summer school at all-white Hopewell High, since their school, Carter G. Woodson, didn't offer summer classes. When they were denied entry, Harris filed a discrimination suit in federal district court. In August, the judge agreed with them, and Hopewell High became integrated. Nevertheless, the Encyclopedia Virginia noted that "as late as 1965, fewer than 12,000 of the approximately 235,000 black students in Virginia went to desegregated schools."

Still, more than ever, separate but equal was dying a slow death.

Many Black students were interviewed years later about their experiences and recalled "the fear, verbal abuse and other indignities they suffered when they ventured into all-white schools." At the same time, political leaders described how Virginia took drastic measures in a vain effort to prevent integration. "It tore Virginia apart and, tragically, the harm will never be understood," said attorney Marsh, who battled racists during the fight to integrate the schools.

Harris expected the process to take time. He saw the difficulty of this transition as necessary to social progress. "When you plant a crop," he explained, "you've got to get the weeds out, and it's hard work, but later on, you get a harvest. My sons and the other kids were planting seeds, and the seeds materialized."

Education was only one prong in his efforts to remove racial restrictions. Protests had placed him outside the system. His next goal was to elbow into the power structure. He had already garnered posts statewide. In 1964, he was named [to the] Virginia Council on Human Relations (VCHR), one of twelve state Councils on Human Relations established by the Southern Regional Council of Atlanta, Georgia. Cofounded in 1955 by the Reverend Wyatt Tee Walker and Martha Elizabeth Hode, the VCHR tried "to prevent human relations conflicts and solve existing problems by organizing local residents in numerous communities."

The group, which never totaled more than 1,200 members, was countered by the Defenders of State Sovereignty, which boasted maybe 3,000 members. Harris caused a hubbub by moving his organization to a Quaker meetinghouse in a residential area in Richmond. Neighbors objected. The city zoning board agreed with the protests, essentially shutting down the VCHR, according to Jay Worrell, who succeeded Harris as director. The organization was revived later and still exists.

In 1968, Harris helped coordinate the "Poor People's Campaign" and "Resurrection City" in Washington, D.C. King had initiated the campaign as the next step in his civil rights platform. The first was integration; the second focused on finding jobs, income and housing for the needy. King called for an "economic bill of rights," funded with $30 billion from the federal government to guarantee annual income while providing jobs and housing.

After King's death, followers decided to continue his efforts and erected a community dubbed Resurrection City on the mall in Washington. Disparaged as a "trash-strewn" gumbo by *Time* magazine, the shantytown briefly hosted poor African Americans, Hispanics and Native Americans from around the country, along with a few whites, but was razed by government officials after surviving barely six weeks. Despite its short duration, the campaign did have some success: The U.S. Department of Agriculture coughed up $20 million more for food stamps and called on more countries to distribute food to the poor. Restrictive eligibility requirements for welfare were pared back. At the same time, the government and employers boosted hiring.

Abernathy, who succeeded King, went to jail after he and some 250 other protestors invaded the Capitol. Abernathy fasted during his twenty-day stay and called for economic boycotts, but only one city—Olympia, Washington—came up with a miniature Resurrection City. It didn't endure long, either.

Instead, Black activists like Harris began to concentrate on worming their way into positions of authority where they could make a real difference. Harris made his first foray by being appointed to the Virginia Advisory Committee to the U.S. Commission on Civil Rights, which dealt with the federal government's role in the desegregation of public schools.

The Reverend Curtis W. Harris Sr. addresses a crowd on June 16, 1982. *Courtesy of Andrew Shannon.*

This kind of exposure meant some unwanted attention. Harris said that someone "threw a Molotov cocktail through my living room window." It didn't explode. Neither did one thrown through Harris's Snack Bar, his small restaurant located next door to the house. A cross had been left on his lawn two weeks earlier. It didn't burn, according to a published report in the *Hopewell News*, because of a fuse malfunction.

Harris, naturally, called the police. "When I complained about it," he recalled, "the chief of police said, 'Curtis Harris ought to expect that.'" Chief Eugene Minter, onetime president of the Virginia Association of Police Chiefs, added that an investigation had been "fruitless. Nobody knows anything," he told the local newspaper. "If they did, they'd never say."

His comments did not go over well after being picked up by United Press International. "He tried to get out of it, but they wouldn't let him out of it. It went all over the country," Harris said. Harris then asked the governor for assistance, but the resulting investigation was eventually dropped. "The governor sent a letter saying that they were investigating, but they've never made a report on the investigation," Harris said.

That kind of futile, frustrating effort to achieve justice further underlined the reality of Black existence: Black people held no power. Civil rights leaders attacked that problem from two directions: voting and politics.

Black leaders had recognized for decades that voting was one of the best paths to equality. All-white primaries had been declared illegal by the Supreme Court in the 1927 *Nixon v. Herndon* decision. President Franklin Roosevelt had signaled his support for increased Black voting after his election in 1932. In 1935, Virginia activists founded the Petersburg League to push for African American voter registration. That led to the statewide Virginia Voters League, which was set up in 1941 during a conference of the Virginia Teachers Association. Backed by the NAACP, the league tried to educate potential Black voters and encourage them to overcome state-imposed barriers to voting.

An annual report from the Virginia Voters League in the 1940s, titled *The Voting Status of Negroes in Virginia*, documented increased Black involvement in the voting process. At the same time, Black leaders were pushing to reform education. In 1940, future Supreme Court justice Thurgood Marshall, attorney Oliver W. Hill and the NAACP legal team got the Fourth Circuit Court of Appeals to agree in *Alston v. Board of Education of the City of Norfolk* that "qualified and similarly assigned black and white teachers in Norfolk, Virginia, schools violated the due process and equal protection clauses of the Fourteenth Amendment to the Constitution." It was one of the first steps toward the 1954 *Brown v. Topeka Board of Education* decision.

By 1948, when Harris was only twenty-four, fifty leading southern activists met at Monticello, Thomas Jefferson's restored home, to sign a declaration on civil rights calling for "freedom from any discrimination bounded by law."

Sixteen years later, Harris was taking that argument into the political realm, the flip side of the equality effort. "We always considered trying to get people inside, to see if we could perfect something," he said.

Over the years, Harris ran for a seat on the city council as well as the state legislature, with no success. "I started to run for elected offices before the Voting Rights Act was adopted [in 1964]," Harris said. "I knew that I was not going to win the election, but every time I ran, more African-Americans became involved and became registered voters. That was one of the reasons why I was running."

Harris's results did not match up to his efforts. "I started in the early 1960s," Harris said. "I ran seven times for city council and lost. In the meantime, I was running for other offices, like the state legislature."

Black candidates were elected elsewhere. In 1966, after the $3.50 Virginia poll tax was finally eliminated, Blacks won city council seats in Richmond, Petersburg and Fredericksburg. Harris was not so fortunate, but then again, he didn't take on a lightweight in that campaign. His target was state senator Garland "Peck" Gray, whose family owned a huge land development company and who had become the central opponent of integration in Virginia. Gray was "one of the most powerful and influential men in the Commonwealth," according to the Virginia Historical Society.

A strong supporter of U.S. senator Byrd, an avowed segregationist, Gray was handpicked to run a legislative committee appointed to create the laws in opposition to the *Brown v. Topeka Board of Education* decision. That legislation was later overturned by the U.S. Supreme Court. Known as the Gray Commission, the legislative committee released a report in January 1955 that boldly stated its objectives to create a legal process "designed to prevent enforced integration of the races in the public schools of Virginia."

Attorney David Mays, counsel for the commission, wrote in his diary that Gray told him that "the art of [the report] is to recognize the binding force of the Supreme Court decision while destroying its effect, at least at present, in the counties having heavy Negro populations."

Gray is credited with holding up full integration in Virginia until 1970. He also drew plenty of support. He was elected to the state legislature on two separate occasions from 1948 to 1971 and was succeeded by his son, Elmon.

Harris found the longtime senator unbeatable. "Ben Ragsdale was my campaign manager," he said. "We tried to unseat Peck Gray, but we were not successful. So, I tried working at it almost full time. And what else is coming up, I am running. I ran for congressional office, for the state legislature, and I ran for the city council, for the city council seven times, and I was not able to succeed."

The passage of the Voting Rights Act in 1964 gave him hope. "After we got the Voting Rights Act, then I started to run seriously, but I could not win in spite of my efforts," Harris said. "By this time, I picked up a few white votes when I would run. But, we had [an] at-large system, and I couldn't win with the at-large system. By this time, the African-American population had increased, but it still was not enough. Plus, we were isolated in the Black community. Every time I would run, the system would not allow me to have enough votes. I would have mostly Black votes."

That was to be expected. Sociologists noted that, for years, at-large election schemes were used by white Democrats in the South to dilute the influence of Black voters or simply to disenfranchise them. Basically, voters across the city would vote to fill seats rather than voting for candidates representing designated areas, giving the white majority guaranteed control. The U.S. Justice Department finally upended this approach in the 1960s and 1970s by forcing cities like Richmond and Petersburg to convert to ward-based elections.

"The ACLU in Richmond started to help me," Harris said. "We were helping other jurisdictions to deal with the at-large system. The U.S. Commission on Civil Rights had a study made to find out why Curtis Harris couldn't get elected to the city council, and why he couldn't get elected to Congress, and why he didn't get elected to the state legislature. The study showed that it was because I was African-American and would not yield to the ideas of the white community."

The report also included comments from city officials, including Mayor Tom Blunt. His written answer to why Harris lost was that he was not fit to be a member of the city council, even though he spent eight years on the city planning commission and was its chairman until being elected to the council. Harris didn't forget that comment. He even kept a book given him by the city commission with that letter in it.

When Harris was finally elected to the city council, Blunt lost at the same time. "I had a chance to tell him. I said, 'Tom, you lied. You said that I was not fit to be a member of the city council, and now I am on the council and you are not on the council. You lost your election.'" After becoming mayor, Harris again reminded Blunt of the previous lie. "He played it off as a joke," Harris said.

Harris won his seat after the ACLU filed suit in federal court to get rid of the at-large system in Hopewell. Initially, the results were bittersweet. For years, Harris was the lone Black resident to run for office in Hopewell. Once the court forced the city into a ward system, Harris said white politicians found a Black candidate, C. Ray Edmonds, to run. Harris won the suit, but Edmonds was elected and got 80 percent of the vote for an at-large seat.

"While we were in court, they elected Edmonds, hoping that we'll go away, that the law would protect them. They were thinking that 'now we got us an African-American, so they can't say that we wouldn't allow African-Americans to be elected,'" Harris said.

That subterfuge failed. Soon after, as Harris's case dragged through federal court, city officials offered a compromise. The city was split into five wards with two at-large seats. Harris was in Ward 2, the largest and least-populated ward. However, 75 percent of the Black community lived there. In 1986, Harris finally was seated on the Hopewell City Council. He won

Mayor Harris and councilman Jeffery Fitch consider an issue during a meeting of the Hopewell City Council. *Used with permission from the Valentine Corporation.*

with more than 75 percent of the votes cast. Harris said, "Black folks were voting for me all along."

Ironically, Edmonds lost in a ward that was 80 percent white. Harris said city attorney Carl Turner told him that white voters rejected the idea of two African Americans on city council. "One nigger is enough," Harris said he was informed.

Harris had no illusions what animosity he faced taking office. Other officials made their feelings clear in print. "Let's face it: He's a controversial figure," said councilwoman Barbara A. Leadbetter, the only incumbent to win reelection in 1986. "I've had several callers this morning, and they're just scared to death that he's on [the] council now." She was more optimistic than her constituents. "I'm hoping he won't use the City Council as a vehicle," she told the local newspaper.

Paul Karnes, the commission's vice chairman, didn't believe Harris would, either. "I was apprehensive about serving with him at first, because I knew he was a racially motivated person," Karnes said. "But his politics have not been a factor at all. I've been pleasantly surprised." After talking with Harris, Leadbetter felt more comfortable with him, too. "I feel certain that he will put his best effort forward," she said.

That's all Harris ever did. It's a technique that resonated with voters. He was reelected for sixteen straight years. "I've been confronted three times during my stay on council, twice by Blacks and one white," Harris said. "I've whopped them all."

Eventually, he also forced the city to drop the at-large system completely. "I threatened to take them to court again," Harris said. "They hired a lawyer to tell them what chance they had to win against me if I go back to court again. The lawyer did some research and gave them the report that they would have less than a 25 percent chance to win against me. So that's how the council agreed to have an all-ward system, and we had another ward."

Hopewell officials knew full well that Harris was serious when he threatened lawsuits. Shortly after Harris was elected to city council, one official complained to the local newspaper, "He's cost us millions of dollars, and now he's going to be one of us."

While campaigning successfully, Harris found time to picket a local supermarket that, he said, stocked South African products and to demand a TV station hire more Black employees. The year before, he joined a sit-in at the End Zone, a gentleman's club/sports bar in Hopewell.

Harris remained on the council and served as the first Black mayor in the town's history from 1994 to 1998. That created some strange bedfellows, since mayors were chosen by a vote of the council members.

"There were two African-Americans on the council and five white

Rev. Curtis W. Harris Sr. talks with two fellow councilmembers after being elected the first Black mayor of Hopewell, Virginia. *Used with permission from the Valentine Corporation.*

persons," Harris said. "The fellow who had already been mayor for four years wanted to run again. We had one real racist on the council, but he didn't like the white person who was running. He called me up and told me that, if I wanted to be the mayor, he would support me. That sent some shock waves through me, but that's what he said. The African-American [on the council] said he would support me. Another person who wanted to be vice mayor said he would support me if he could just be the vice mayor. So that was four votes. When I had four votes, that's all I needed. When they found out that I had four votes, they agreed to make it unanimous. So that's how I got to be the mayor of the city. I served four years."

To Harris, his election to head of city government marked the culmination of his forty years of social activism. "I was selected by five white persons," he noted. "I think the Lord had something to do with it."

Harris recognized immediately how his role had changed in the community. Harris told the Petersburg newspaper that his election to the council will change his approach rather than his message. "I have a vote now. Before, I've always been on the outside. Now everything I do in the city will be initiated from within."

Harris's social engineering, however, did not cease when he became a member of the establishment. "My past challenges

Surrounded by paperwork, Rev. Curtis W. Harris Sr. presides over a council meeting as mayor of Hopewell, Virginia. *Used with permission from the Valentine Corporation.*

to Hopewell's government, although initiated on behalf of the poor or the Black, have been conducted with the good of all Hopewell residents in mind," Harris said.

One effort linked his past with his present. For years, Harris had tried to get the council to approve placing a statue of Dr. Martin Luther King Jr. in the downtown Ashford Civic Plaza, which already hosted a marker to commemorate the Confederacy and the U.S. Government bakery that once fed troops and the Union Army of the James River. Then, over his objections, the council voted for an alternative plan, minus the statue of King. Harris refused to go along and publicly spoke out. Properly embarrassed, the council approved the statue.

To get funds for the project, Harris approached the local John Randolph Foundation, which is "a community-based foundation working to improve the health and quality of life for residents of Hopewell and surrounding areas through grants and scholarships." It's named for an early American statesman born in Roanoke in 1773 who owned slaves and was an outspoken advocate of the institution. "The question of slavery, as it is called, is to us a question of life and death....You will find no instance in history where two distinct races have occupied the soil except in the relation of master and slave," Randolph said. Harris ran into an old combatant at the organization: former mayor Blunt was president of Randolph's grant committee. Harris didn't get the money.

He also did not give up. More than four decades of facing entrenched opposition had hardened him to rejection. "There are two Black women who are on the foundation now," he said in 2003, "so we're going to have a big fight going on with that. We're going to put that statue in the plaza. If we can't put it in the plaza, we're going to put up a statue of Martin Luther King if I have to put it in my yard."

That wasn't necessary. A seven-foot bronze statue dedicated to King now stands in the Ashford Civic Plaza. It features a bust of King with arms folded across his chest and the words:

On March 29, 1962 Dr. King
appeared in Hopewell
District Court as a
defender of civil rights
in America.

"Injustice anywhere is a
threat to justice
everywhere."

Dedicated April 4, 2004

That success emboldened Harris and made sure his retirement was still a few years in the future. In 1987, he led a march against discrimination in Colonial Heights. According to published reports, "More than 600 people, most of them Black, marched through the nearly all-white city, demanding jobs and equal housing opportunities." Colonial Heights, located next to Petersburg, about nine miles from Hopewell, was predominately white. Only 37 Blacks were identified among the city's 16,509 residents in the 1980 census.

Harris, who had just won his first election to Hopewell's city council, said the march idea developed while participating in a protest in all-white, rural Forsyth County, located north of Atlanta, Georgia. "We concluded that it was ironic, and a question of our sincerity, to go way down to Georgia to march against fear and intimidation and not raise our voices against it in

Colonial Heights," Harris said. He agreed that Forsythe was different from urban Colonial Heights. "The bottom line is that just as much effort is being put forth in Colonial Heights to keep it only white as there is in Forsyth County," he explained. "We don't want to do anything bad to Colonial Heights. We simply want it to be an open community."

No one was arrested, but marchers were heckled by crowds waving Confederate flags and jeering. Harris taped a list of demands on city hall at the end of the march.

The protest was countered by one about a week later led by the short-lived Southern National Front (SNF), which promoted the idea of separate nations for the races. In the SNF-sponsored march, about one hundred people paraded for a mile, shouting, "White power." Police chief John Wofford said that police couldn't identify anyone from Colonial Heights. The SNF, founded by two members of the White Patriot Party, held ten marches that year and then disappeared.

Today, Colonial Heights is about 13 percent African American, according to the most recent census figures.

Harris continued on. In 1994, he joined a longtime local activist, Milton Reid, and hundreds of other activists to protest Colonial Williamsburg's historic reenactment of a slave auction. The auction was part of a three-day celebration of the coronation of King George III, the man against whom the colonists rebelled. SCLC objected to the auction, insisting it "trivialized and degraded African-American history." More than two thousand people showed up on the Duke of Gloucester Street to watch four slaves being "sold."

At the same time, the national office of the NAACP and the Virginia state chapter released a statement saying that "Colonial Williamsburg is perpetuating the fallacies of denying the true depiction of history and glorifying the horrors and humiliations of the evils of slavery through a one-day event." Brenda Andrews, publisher of the *New Journal and Guide* in Norfolk, Virginia, added that "the institution of slavery was the African holocaust in America. And we must not forget that. We must not make light of it. We must not allow that institution to be sanitized nor sugar coated."

Williamsburg got the message. The organization quickly introduced Black actors into the daily life portrayed in the city. By 1999, Black performers comprised almost 10 percent of the 578-member ensemble. Changes to the performers won the support of the local NAACP for its "extensive treatment of Colonial slavery."

Soon after, back home in Hopewell, Harris was arrested for the last time. Charged with trespassing, he was protesting "inappropriate management practices" at a local skating rink.

In 1996, then seventy-two and still feisty, Harris filed a discrimination complaint against a Fort Lee, Virginia military unit. That year, Fort Lee agreed to end a 1989 suit filed by the NAACP by dropping the requirement that municipal workers must live within the town's borders. The NAACP claimed the rule discriminated against minority group members. Five other communities in the suit had previously settled out of court.

Harris was not through. In 2007, he led a three-block march against the building of an ethanol plant in Hopewell. Harris was not opposed to the Appomattox Bio Energy plant but said its location on the Exeter Site at the southern end of Main Street opened the public to "risk of highly flammable materials and explosive hazards. Hundreds of kids would be exposed to that situation if a plant is put there and an explosion takes place," he said. "Of course, others will be exposed, but kids especially. It makes us very apprehensive to put the plant so close in the neighborhoods."

Rev. Curtis W Harris joined with Andrew Shannon in the 2011 ethanol plant protest. *Courtesy of Andrew Shannon.*

VIRGINIA'S CIVIL RIGHTS HERO CURTIS W. HARRIS SR.

Harris also got the national SCLC to pass a resolution to support his objections, which did not stop the $160 million plant from being built. Then, in 2010, it suffered an explosion linked to faulty equipment.

"Some of the areas I was concerned about, such as safety, are coming to pass. I'm concerned it could happen again on a larger scale," Harris said at the time. "It's in my backyard, and I don't want it in my backyard."

He didn't have to worry. In 2011, the Appomattox Bio Energy plant was put on the market by owner Osage Bio Energy without actually having produced any ethanol. The building was eventually purchased by a British company, with plans to disassemble and ship it overseas for use in a British ethanol plant in northeastern England. Instead, in 2014, Vireol Bio-Energy LLC announced it was reopening the facility, labeling it the biggest ethanol plant on the East Coast. A year later, the company filed for bankruptcy.

Even after a stroke, Harris refused to remain on the sidelines. Andrew Shannon, president of the Peninsula Southern Christian Leadership Conference, invited him to a march in Newport News over a disagreement about that city's hiring policy. Shannon was stunned when Harris showed up in a wheelchair. He remembered Harris couldn't speak clearly but thoughtfully provided copies of his speech for the media. "Everyone still hung onto his words as he spoke," Shannon said. "He brought national and state leaders to Newport News. I'd say, 'Curtis Harris is with me,' people would come."

CHAPTER 8

RECOGNITION

I n 2004, the once-segregated Carter G. Woodson Middle School held a dedication ceremony for the newly renamed Rev. Dr. Curtis W. Harris Sr. Library. Harris was then eighty years old.

He had come a long way in those years, from anonymous poverty to widespread affection and admiration. "I was involved in sit-ins in several places, including Danville, Richmond, Petersburg, and especially in Hopewell," he recalled prior to the dedication ceremony. "Hopewell is a small city, with only about 24,000 people in the whole city. I think at that time about 18 percent of them were African Americans. At one time, we were not able to sit down at the lunch counters, and we were not able to go into the main library. You were not welcome into the library—not only in Hopewell, but in Petersburg, and across Virginia."

Now, a library had been named for him. He was also accepted and appreciated within his community. Then–*Hopewell News* editor Kit Weigel told the *Washington Post* that "even the old-line, traditional whites have come to see his value for the community." No one would have said that in the 1960s.

"Reverend Harris is a pillar of this community," Herbert H. Bragg, the city's intergovernmental director, told the *Richmond Times-Dispatch* in 2011. "He has done a lot of good in the city and throughout the country."

Longtime resident Jim Willcox added, "He was pushing for change, but he understood…that change took time, that things weren't going to change instantly."

Entrance to the
Hopewell high
school library
renamed for Rev.
Curtis W. Harris Sr.
*Courtesy of Jeremy
M. Lazarus.*

Not in Hopewell. Longtime resident and library archivist Jeanie Langford recalled attending Klan rallies in the city. Her father was one of the KKK members Harris had confronted on the city hall steps years before. "I saw my father get up and walk out of a restaurant here in Hopewell when Rev. Harris walked in," she said. "Segregation, when I was young, that was the way it was supposed to be."

Harris made sure that changed. Time also helped alter Harris's image from that of a firebrand to someone deeply concerned about his community. His brother-in-law and frequent campaign manager James Patterson said, "Curtis Harris will be about what he has always been about, but he may be a little wiser than he has been in the past. As you get older, what's down in your heart is the same, but it comes out a little different."

Nothing could reflect the change more than a community ride and rally held on January 22, 2011, in Harris's honor. Sponsored by the Southeast Community Day Planning Committee, the rally included members of various civil rights organizations, the Peninsula Unity Riders and Tight On 2 Wheels motorcycle clubs and religious and community leaders. The gathering was in addition to the annual Dr. Curtis W. Harris Solidarity Lunch held every September. This kind of procession, filled with affection and support, starkly contrasts with the marches through groups of angry whites throwing stones and epithets.

In fact, most everything had changed in the life Curtis Harris knew but his clothes. Harris, naturally, owned "go-to-church" clothes. He had others for protests. During marches in Alabama, he recalled standing in front of a courthouse there. "The sheriff ran us off and it was raining," Harris said.

The high school library, named for the Reverend Curtis W. Harris Sr., contains a small museum dedicated to him. *Courtesy of Jeremy M. Lazarus.*

"We stayed there as long as we could and, finally, we had to leave." The next stop was a clothing store for Harris and his companions. "We were wet through and through," Harris said. He bought a pair of blue jeans and a denim jacket. They became his uniform for the many marches and demonstrations that followed. In the photo of the 1966 rally against the city dump, Harris can be seen wearing his jeans while leading his small band of marchers. The jeans remained in his closet. The scars stayed on his body.

"I was afraid," Harris said. "I'm a human. Every once in a while, as a human, my flesh gets weak, but we got through it. Sometimes I didn't want to do it, but I realized I didn't have any real choice. When you get involved in a civil rights movement of nonviolence, you make yourself available for whatever comes your way."

Some of it was vicious. One beating in Suffolk sent him to Obici Hospital there. "He was in worse shape than when he was coming from Alabama," his youngest son, Michael, recalled. He said that his father was hit numerous times, including a punch to the face strong enough to snap his glasses in half. At the same time, he saw how his father endured the blows and continued on. "I would get angry and always wanted to retaliate," Michael said, "but my father diffused that."

Harris never wavered. "I'm not half as radical as some think," he said after winning his first election, "but I'm radical enough. Some of the injustices we see perpetrated on the people are downright un-Christian. From time to time, I've had to call upon people in authority for certain changes. My style has been to be an advocate, and that won't change."

Wearing his traditional jeans, the Reverend Curtis W. Harris Sr. leads a 1973 protest march. *Courtesy of Swem Library, College of William & Mary.*

As a result, he drew praise from those who had marched with him or reaped the benefits of his efforts. "Curtis Harris will pluck the Establishment's nerves and perhaps will pluck the nerves of some Blacks who are conservative in their views," said the Reverend W. Paul Matthews Jr., executive secretary of the state chapter of the NAACP. "But he does it for a good cause. There is a need for a person of Mr. Harris' style—who has no problem with confrontations."

Even people Harris opposed did not necessarily become enemies. Fort Lee's commanding officer, Lieutenant General Billy K. Solomon, addressed a ceremony to honor Harris, who found it ironic that the man who oversaw the army base that he marched on and filed a suit against spoke favorably of him.

"It was always pleasant working with Curtis because you always knew where you stood. I think he has been a real asset here in Hopewell," said Riley E. Ingram, who joined the Hopewell City Council in 1986 along with Harris and was elected to the Virginia House of Delegates in 1992. "I didn't always agree with Curtis, but even if he disagreed with you, he was never disagreeable," Ingram said then. "He and his wife both are just great people. They are good for the city; they really are." Ingram, who is white, said Harris's work for the city "knows no boundaries, physical or otherwise. He enjoys people, and he enjoys what he is doing. He looks after everyone— not just the people in his ward but all of the people in the city."

"Basically. I've just been a city councilman," Harris agreed. "I get more calls from people concerned about city issues from the white community than the Black community."

In return, he received accolades statewide, including the Outstanding Citizen Award from the Virginia Council of Social Welfare, the Citizen of the Year Award from Delta Omega Chapter, and the Man of the Year Award from the Petersburg Chapter National Association of Negro Business and Professional Women Club. Virginia Union awarded him an honorary doctor of divinity degree along with the Dedicated Service Award. Later, Harris was awarded an honorary doctor of law from Virginia Seminary and College.

The SCLC gave Rev. Harris the Rosa Parks Award, which honors individuals who made "noteworthy contributions to the struggle for human dignity." He also received the organization's Inspirational Award, its Martin Luther King Jr. Community Service Award and the Unmatched Determination Award.

On a national level, Harris received the American Century Award from the Washington Times Foundation for reflecting "the finest qualities of faith, family, freedom and community service."

The U.S. Department of Housing and Urban Development gave Harris a Recognition of Excellence Award. He was given a Certificate of Service Award from the U.S. Commission on Civil Rights. Along with Secretary of State Colin Powell, Harris was recognized during the 11th Anniversary Celebration of Outstanding Achievements by African-Americans.

On the state level, Harris won the Jon D. Strother Human Rights Award, named for first president of the Virginia Association of Human Rights Commissioners, now known as the Virginia Association for Human Rights.

Other recognition included the Support of Children Award from the City of Hopewell School Board, the Unmatched Determination Award from the national board of the SCLC, the Lifetime Service to Fellowmen Award from the Surry County Citizens Forum and the Real Dream Award from the Martin Luther King Jr. Family Life Institute.

Four more high points were achieved in the last decade of Harris's life. In 2008, Harris and his grandson, Curtis III, attended the inauguration of Barack Obama, the first African American president. They also joined the prayer breakfast the following morning.

The Reverend Curtis and Ruth Harris. *Used with permission from the* Richmond Times-Dispatch.

In addition, in 2008, the government also approved the creation of a nonprofit organization in Hopewell called the C.W. Harris Empowerment Center, which is designed to host "activities and programs created to empower the Black community in becoming productive citizens."

In addition, the name of the road where Rev. Harris has lived for most of his life in Hopewell was changed from Terminal to Rev. C.W. Harris Street in 2014. The *Hopewell News* reported, "Now, his legacy will be honored with the street name change, a street where Harris lived and housed his heart and family."

The main post office in Hopewell now also bears his name.

At the same time, Harris's late wife was honored, too. Nearby Booker Street was renamed for her. Previously, Ruth Harris received an honorary doctorate of humane letters from Virginia University in 1986. In 2007, the National Southern Christian Leadership Conference named her one of the first recipients of the Faithful Servant Award. She was also appointed by the Hopewell City Council to serve on the Senior Citizens Commission from 1981 to 1985.

Letters and other documents from Rev. Harris's life have been collected in the Swem Library at the College of William & Mary.

For Harris, all of the family awards and recognition were nice, but the results were more significant.

Harris spoke of his lifelong effort from a religious perspective. "If I can help somebody as I pass along. If I can cheer somebody with a word or a song; if I can show somebody they're traveling wrong, then my living shall not be in vain," he said, repeating the words of a favorite gospel song, "If I Can Help Somebody."

> *If I can help somebody, as I pass along,*
> *If I can cheer somebody, with a word or song,*
> *If I can show somebody, how they're travelling wrong,*
> *Then my living shall not be in vain.*

Chorus:
My living shall not be in vain,
Then my living shall not be in vain
If I can help somebody, as I pass along,
Then my living shall not be in vain.

If I can do my duty, as a good man ought,
If I can bring back beauty, to a world up wrought,
If I can spread love's message, as the Master taught,
Then my living shall not be in vain.

Chorus:
If I can help somebody, as I pass along,
If I can cheer somebody, with a word or song,
If I can show somebody, how they're travelling wrong,
Then my living shall not be in vain.

Chorus:
My living shall not be in vain,
Then my living shall not be in vain
If I can help somebody, as I pass along,
Then my living shall not be in vain.

If I can do my duty, as a good man ought,
If I can bring back beauty, to a world up wrought,
If I can spread love's message, as the Master taught,
Then my living shall not be in vain.

Harris also drew on the Bible for inspiration. "As the little lad freely gave of his lunch, two fishes and five barley loaves, which was magnified by Christ and became the supper for thousands, so does every young person have something that Christ can use to supply the needs of others," Harris said.

At the same time, he recognized that the journey was not complete. "I don't think racism is dead. I think it is very much alive, but I do think things are better," Harris said. "Now we are dealing with diversity."

That will require more effort, more willingness to confront problems head on. Despite strokes in 1992 and 2011, he remained ready to continue, although he did retire from the Hopewell City Council in 2012 prior to the end of his seventh term. "It's been a long run. It wasn't about anybody hassling me. I knew I had to come out at some point," he said at the time.

When Harris left the council, he was no longer an active minister. He first served as pastor at First Baptist Bermuda Hundred in Chester, Virginia, before moving to Union Baptist Church in Hopewell and Gilfield Baptist Church in Ivor, Virginia, in 1961. Ivor and Hopewell are about forty-one miles apart. He retired from Gilfield in 1994 and from Union Baptist in 2007.

That doesn't mean he thought his legacy was complete. "No one really knows that they're making history. They do what they think needs to be done. I did the best I could," Harris said. "And there are a lot of things left to be done."

He then quoted a line from Matthew (17:20) that also appeared on his Facebook page:

> *I tell you the truth, if you have faith as small as a mustard seed, you can say to this mountain, "Move from here to there" and it will move. Nothing will be impossible for you.*

When he started, "everything was segregated," Harris said in a 1991 interview. "There was so much going on which we didn't like. People were being stepped on. Our action could have been violent or nonviolent. We chose the path of nonviolent action." Harris said the Civil Rights Movement was about justice. "Not every law is just. Certainly, the segregation laws were not just. In these circumstances," he said, "there have to be special people who will call into question the laws which are on the books. Direct action was our response to great injustice."

The effort was hard. "In our struggles," Harris said, "we were faced with cruelty on a daily basis. The segregation laws, themselves inhuman, were enforced with police dogs, billy clubs and fire hoses. These things were used to beat us down. But because we were doing what was just," he continued, "the authorities could not stop us."

"He was an excellent father and a brilliant man, and as his child the only regret that I have is that I did not start listening to him earlier in life," his son, Michael, said.

"To me," said Hopewell's mayor, Jackie Shornak, after Rev. Harris died in 2017, "he was so impressive. I admired him so much—what passion to have in doing something good for people!"

Added Shornak, who was a student at Hopewell High School when it was desegregated, "It's admirable what he and his whole family did, and what a miracle he was to bring the civil rights movement out to the public and to Hopewell."

CHRONOLOGY

1924
Born

1944
Attended Virginia Union

1946
Married Ruth Jones

1956
Licensed as a minister at Union Baptist Church, Hopewell

1959
Ordained as a minister at Union Baptist Church

1960
Organized the Hopewell Improvement Association, an affiliate of the
    Southern Christian Leadership Conference (SCLC) and was elected
    vice president
Arrested for trespassing and sentenced to sixty days in jail for sit-in at the
    segregated Georges' Drugstore in Hopewell
Led a protest against the segregated swimming pool and cemetery in
    Hopewell

1961

Became a member of the National Board of Southern Christian
  Leadership Conference
Cited for contempt by the Boatwright Committee of the Virginia General
  Assembly for not revealing the names of other SCLC members nor
  responding to the questions asked by the committee
Named pastor at the Union Baptist Church in Hopewell and the Gillfield
  Baptist Church in Ivor

1962

Accompanied by Dr. Martin Luther King Jr. to court for the contempt trial
  in Hopewell

1963

Elected president of the Virginia State Unit of the SCLC
Led a march against discrimination and was arrested in Danville, Virginia
Two sons, Curtis Jr. and Kenneth, became the first African American
  students to attend Hopewell High School
Joined King in the March on Washington and witnessed the delivery of the
  "I Have a Dream" speech

1964

Became the director of the Virginia Council on Human Relations

1965

Marched with King from Selma to Montgomery

1966

Protested placement of a landfill in Hopewell
Confronted Ku Klux Klan on the steps of Hopewell's city hall

1967

Cross erected in front yard, but it did not burn
Bombs thrown through the picture window of his home and neighboring
  restaurant, but did not explode

1968
Worked on Poor People's Campaign and Resurrection City in
    Washington, D.C.
Selected to serve on the Virginia Advisory Committee to the U.S.
    Commission on Civil Rights
Attended King's funeral in Atlanta, Georgia

1969
Arrested after being beaten in Suffolk for protesting discrimination

1971
Outstanding Citizenship Award from the Virginia Council on Social
    Welfare
Citizen of the Year Award from Alpha Kappa Alpha Sorority, Delta
    Omega Chapter
Man of the Year Award from the Petersburg chapter of the National
    Association of Negro Business and Professional Women

1972
Awarded an honorary doctor of divinity from the Virginia University

1978
Received the Dedicated Service Award from Virginia State University

1979
Reorganized the Virginia State Unit of the SCLC

1981
Received the Rosa Parks Award from the national SCLC
Received the Inspirational Award from the Virginia SCLC

1982
Received Centennial Community Recognition Award from the Virginia SCLC

1983
Received Martin Luther King Jr. Community Service Award from the
    Virginia SCLC
Filed lawsuit requiring Hopewell to replace its at-large system with wards
Awarded an honorary doctor of law from the Virginia University

1984
Received the Recognition of Excellence Award from the U.S. Department
of Housing and Urban Development

1986
Elected to the Hopewell City Council after seven attempts

1987
Led a march against discrimination in Colonial Heights

1989
Received the Outstanding Achievement Award from Hopewell

1990
Led march on Fort Lee against employment discrimination

1992
Received the Unmatched Determination Award from the national SCLC
Received Martin Luther King Jr. Legacy Award from Alpha Phi Alpha
Fraternity
Received Appreciation Award from Emporia Greenville SCLC

1994
Elected first African American mayor of the City of Hopewell

1995
Received a Certificate of Service from the U.S. Commission on Civil
Rights
Received a Lifetime Service to Fellowmen Award from Surry County
Citizens Forum

1996
Filed complaint against the command center for Fort Lee, for discrimination

1998
Received the Real Dream Award from Martin Luther King Jr. Family Life
Institute
Resigned as president of the Virginia SCLC

2000
Received an American Century Award from the Washington Times
   Foundation

2004
Carter G. Woodson Middle School Library dedicated in his honor

2005
Elected national vice president of the National SCLC

2007
Led a march against the building of an ethanol plant in Hopewell
Retired as pastor of Union Baptist Church

2017
Died

BIBLIOGRAPHY

INTRODUCTION

Warren, Michael. "National Urban League Finds State of Black America Is Grim." *Florida Courier*, April 12, 2022. https://www.flcourier.com/news/national-urban-league-finds-state-of-black-america-is-grim/article_1316b83e-ba78-11ec-af4d-470351a4bf08.html.

Kaiser Family Foundation. "Race and Ethnicity in 2001: Attitudes, Perceptions and Experiences." Kaiser Family Foundation, September 1, 2001. www.kff.org/kaiserpolls/3143-index.cfm.

Joint Economic Committee of Congress. *The Economic State of Black America in 2020.* May 2020. https://www.jec.senate.gov/public/_cache/files/ccf4dbe2-810a-44f8-b3e7-14f7e5143ba6/economic-state-of-black-america-2020.pdf.

Virginia Center for Digital History. "An Act to Preserve Racial Integrity." http://www2.vcdh.virginia.edu/lewisandclark/students/projects/monacans/Contemporary_Monacans/racial.html.

Encyclopedia Virginia. "Racial Integrity Laws (1924–1930)." www.encyclopedia virginia .org/Racial_Integrity_Laws_of_the_1920s.

CHAPTER 1

Dendron

City-Data.com. "Dendron, Virginia." www.city-data.com/city/Dendron-Virginia.html.

Huber, Jack. "The Surry Lumber Company—Logs, Locomotives and Lumber." *Virginia Forests* (Winter 2000). http://www.rootsweb.ancestry.com/~vaschs/SLCfinal.htm.

Donnell, Kelly. "Down Home in Dendron." *Cooperative Living*, 2009.

Black Families

Digital History. "Building the Black Community: The Family." 2003.

Surrey County, Virginia

Surrey County Historical Society. http://surrycounty.pastperfectonline.com.

Chicago Riot

History.com. "The Red Summer of 1919." Last updated August 6, 2020. https://www.history.com/topics/black-history/chicago-race-riot-of-1919.

Hopewell, Virginia

"Hopewell, Virginia." History and Hopewell Facts, 2009. https://hopewellva.gov/city-history/.

Dent, Edward E. *Race Relations in Hopewell, VA, 1635–1932*. Brunswick, ME: Brunswick Publishing, 1992.

Lee, Lauranett L. *Making the American Dream Work: A Cultural History of African Americans in Hopewell, Virginia*. New York: Morgan James Publishing, 2008.

New York Times. "Fire Destroys Du Pont City." December 10, 1915. https://www.nytimes.com/1915/12/10/archives/fire-destroys-du-pont-city-looter-lynched-flames-sweep-hopewell-va.html.

Progress-Index. "Hopewell Born among the Guns of War." February 15, 2015. https://www.progress-index.com/story/opinion/editorials/2015/02/06/hopewell-born-among-guns-war/35214724007/.

Richmond (VA) Times-Dispatch. "Riot in Hopewell Quelled by Troops; Three Men Shot." October 5, 1918.

Lynching

University of Missouri–Kansas City School of Law. "Lynchings: By Year and Race." http://law2.umkc.edu/faculty/projects/ftrials/shipp/lynchingyear.html.

Religious Revivals

Carpenter, Joel A. *Revive Us Again: The Reawakening of Religious Fundamentalism.* London: Oxford University Press, 1999.

Virginia Racial Laws

Tartar, Brent. "Lawes Divine Morall and Martiall." Encyclopedia Virginia. https://encyclopediavirginia.org/entries/lawes-divine-morall-and-martiall/.

Race Relations in the 1930s

McCune, Grace, Miriam McCommons and Jennifer Briggs. "Views of Race Relations by the 1930's Society of Whites and Blacks." University of Georgia, 2004. https://sclfind.libs.uga.edu/sclfind/view?docId=ead/ms1478. xml;query=;brand=default.

Library of Congress. "Race Relations in the 1930s and 1940s." Accessed December 17, 2018. http://www.loc.gov/teachers/classroommaterials/presentationsandactivities/presentations/timeline/depwwii/race/.

Charles Houston

NAACP. "Charles Hamilton Houston." https://naacp.org/find-resources/history-explained/civil-rights-leaders/charles-hamilton-houston.

Slavery; Carter Woodson High School

Hopewell News, October 18, 1999.

CHAPTER 2

Amendments

BlackHistory.com. "Black History." 2007.

Justice Lemuel Shaw

Mass.gov. "Portraits in Massachusetts Law: Lemuel Shaw." https://www.mass. gov/news/portraits-in-massachusetts-law-lemuel-shaw.

Levy, Leonard. "Lemuel Shaw: America's Greatest Magistrate." *Villanova Law Review* 7, no. 3 (Spring 1962): 389–406.

Law Library—American Law and Legal Information. "Roberts v. City of Boston: 1848–49." https://law.jrank.org/pages/2500/Roberts-v-City-Boston-1848-49. html.

John Underwood

Tarter, Brent, and the Dictionary of Virginia Biography. "John C. Underwood (1809–1873)." Encyclopedia Virginia. December 13, 2015. https://www. encyclopediavirginia.org/Underwood_John_C_1809-1873.

Slaughterhouse Cases

'Lectric Law Library. "Slaughter-House Cases." https://www.lectlaw.com/files/ case30.htm.

Louisiana Separate Car Act

Encyclopedia Britannica. "Louisiana Separate Car Act." https://www.britannica. com/topic/Louisiana-Separate-Car-Act.

Albion Winegar Tourgée

Powell, William S., ed. "Albion Winegar Tourgée, 1838–1905." In *Dictionary of North Carolina Biography*. Chapel Hill: University of North Carolina Press, 1979. Accessed via Documenting the American South, https://docsouth.unc.edu/church/tourgee/bio.html.

Plessy v. Ferguson

PBS Home Programs: American Experience. "Jim Crow and Plessy v. Ferguson." 2006. https://www.pbs.org/tpt/slavery-by-another-name/themes/jim-crow/.

Judge Henry Billings Brown

F. Helminski. "Henry Billings Brown." In *Oxford Companion to the Supreme Court of the United States*, 2nd ed., edited by Kermit L. Hall. Oxford University Press, 2005.

Judge John Harlan

King, Gilbert. "The Great Dissenter and His Half-Brother." *Smithsonian Magazine*, December 20, 2011. https://www.smithsonianmag.com/history/the-great-dissenter-and-his-half-brother-10214325/.
Leitch, Alexander. "John Harlan." In *A Princeton Companion*. Princeton, NJ: Princeton University Press, 1978.

Disenfranchising Black Voters

Tartar, Brent. "Disenfranchising Black Voters." Encyclopedia Virginia. www.encyclopediavirginia.org/Disfranchisement.
Tucker, T. Nicole. "White Supremacy & African-American Resistance in Charlottesville, Virginia 1900–1925." University of Virginia. www2.vcdh.virginia.edu/afam/politics/legislation.html.

Charles Houston

NAACP. "Charles Hamilton Houston." Accessed December 18, 2018. https://www.naacp.org/naacp-history-charles-hamilton-houston/.

CHAPTER 3

Lynching

Daily National Intelligencer (Washington, DC). "Nat Turner Finally Captured and Identified!" November 7, 1831. Accessed via the Mitchell Archives. https://mitchellarchives.com/nat-turner-finally-captured-and-identified.htm.

Education

Jackson, Alice J., and Gregory Swanson. "Breaking Tradition: Separate but Not Equal." University of Virginia Special Collections Library, 2009.
Parker, Priya N. "Storming the Gates of Knowledge: A Documentary History of Desegregation and Coeducation in Jefferson's Academic Village." Woodson Projects. State of Virginia, 2004. https://wikious.com/en/University_of_Virginia.

Desegregation

Wallenstein, Peter. "Desegregation in Higher Education." Encyclopedia Virginia, July 26, 2022. https://encyclopediavirginia.org/entries/desegregation-in-higher-education/.

Eugenics

Racial Integrity Act

Wolfe, Brendan. "Racial Integrity Laws (1924–1930)." Encyclopedia Virginia, February 25, 2021. http://www.EncyclopediaVirginia.org/Racial_Integrity_Laws_of_the_1920s.

Lombardo, Paul. "Miscegenation, Eugenics, and Racism: Historical Footnotes to *Loving v. Virginia.*" *U.C. Davis Law Review* 21, no. 2 (Winter 1988): 425. https://readingroom.law.gsu.edu/cgi/viewcontent.cgi?referer=&httpsredir=1&article=1967&context=faculty_pub.

Encyclopedia.com. "Stoddard, T. Lothrop." Accessed 2011. http://www.encyclopedia.com/article-1G2-2831200360/stoddard-t-lothrop.html.

PBS. "Eugenics Movement Reaches Its Height: 1923." 1998. http://www.pbs.org/wgbh/aso/databank/entries/dh23eu.html.

Earnest Sevier Cox

Smith, Douglas, and the Dictionary of Virginia Biography. "Earnest Sevier Cox (1880–1966)." Encyclopedia Virginia, June 22, 2022. https://www.encyclopediavirginia.org/Cox_Earnest_Sevier_1880-1966.

Racial Laws

Wolfe, Brendan. "Racial Integrity Laws (1924–1930)." Encyclopedia Virginia, February 25, 2021. http://www.EncyclopediaVirginia.org/Racial_Integrity_Laws_of_the_1920s.

Sir Francis Galton

Aubert-Marson, Dominique. "Sir Francis Galton: The Father of Eugenics." *Med Sci* 25, no. 6–7 (June–July 2009): 641–45. https://doi.org/10.1051/medsci/2009256-7641.

Dr. Walter Plecker

Cox, John Woodrow. "Death of 'A Devil': The White Supremacist Got Hit by a Car. His Victims Celebrated." *Washington Post*, August 2, 2017. https://www.washingtonpost.com/news/retropolis/wp/2017/08/02/death-of-a-devil-the-white-supremacist-got-hit-by-a-car-his-victims-celebrated/.

Fiske, Warren. "The Black and White World of Walter Ashby Plecker." *Virginian Pilot*, August 18, 2004. https://www.pilotonline.com/history/article_654a811f-213f-5d97-a469-51cc43b1a77f.html.

David Starr Jordan

Black, Edwin. "The Horrifying American Roots of Nazi Eugenics." 2010. https://historynewsnetwork.org/article/1796.

Marcuse, Harold. "Eugenics and Euthanasia." University of California, Santa Barbara, 2005. www.history.ucsb.edu/faculty/marcuse/classes/33d/33d05/33d05L07Eugenics.htm.

Black Athletes

Lapchick, Richard. "Breaking the College Color Barrier: Studies in Courage." February 20, 2008. https://www.espn.com/espn/blackhistory2008/columns/story?columnist=lapchick_richard&id=3254974.

Rockefeller Foundation

Georgetown University. "National Information Resource on Ethics and Human Genetics." Bulletin 10A, n.d. https://elsihub.org/grant-abstract/national-information-resource-ethics-and-human-genetics.

Laughlin, Harry H. *Eugenics Record Office Bulletin No. 10A: Report of the Committee to Study and to Report on the Best Practical Means of Cutting Off the Defective Germ-Plasm in the American Population. I. The Scope of the Committee's Work.* Long Island, NY, 1914. https://repository.library.georgetown.edu/handle/10822/556985.

Paul Popenoe

Foulkes, Debbie. "Paul Popenoe (1888–1979) First Marriage Counselor and Eugenicist." Forgotten Newsmakers, 2010. https://forgottennewsmakers.com/2010/10/27/paul-popenoe-1888-1979-first-marriage-counselor-and-eugenicist/.

Oliver Wendell Holmes Jr.

Doerr, Adam. "Three Generations of Imbeciles Are Enough." *Genomics Law Report*, 2009.

Dr. Walter Plecker

Talbot, Tori. "Walter Ashby Plecker (1861–1947)." Encyclopedia Virginia, June 22, 2022. http://www.EncyclopediaVirginia.org/Plecker_Walter_ Ashby_1861-1947.

Wood, Karenne, and Diane Shields. "The Monacan Indians: Our Story." Virginia Projects. State of Virginia, n.d. https://www.worldcat.org/title/monacan-indians-our-story/oclc/44177957

Gilliam, J. Casey. "White and Everything Else: Harry H. Laughlin's Promotion of Dr. Walter A. Plecker's Virginia Racial Integrity Efforts." Lynchburg College, n.d.

Dr. Joseph S. DeLarnette

University of Virginia Health Systems, Claude Moore Health Sciences Library. "Eugenics in Virginia." 2004. https://www.uvm.edu/~lkaelber/eugenics/VA/ VA.html.

Adolf Hitler

Hardin, Peter. "Segregation's Era of 'Science,' Eugenics Altered Lives, Left Mark in Virginia." *Richmond Times-Dispatch.* http://www.timesdispatch.com/.

CHAPTER 4

Hercules Power Company

Funding Universe. "Hercules Power Company." N.d. http://www.fundinguniverse. com/company-histories/hercules-inc-history/.

Allied Chemical. *International Directory of Company Histories.* Vol. 66. St. James, MO: St. James Press, 2004.

Honeywell International. "The History of Honeywell." n.d. https://www. honeywell.com/us/en/company/our-history.

Ruth Jones Harris

Hallman, Randy. "Ruth Jones Harris, Wife of Hopewell Civil-Rights Icon, Dies at 86." *Richmond Times-Dispatch*, May 27, 2011. https://www.richmond.com/entertainment/ruth-jones-harris-wife-of-hopewell-civil-rights-icon-dies/article_3f6cd751-8f6c-59ca-8ed3-02db324d424c.html.

Oliver Hill, Spottswood Robinson

PBS. "Spottswood W. Robinson III (1916–)." 2004. www.pbs.org/beyondbrown/history/spottswood.html.

Executive Order 9981

Harry S. Truman Library and Museum. "Executive Order 9981: Desegregation of the Armed Forces, July 26, 1948." https://www.trumanlibrary.gov/library/research-files/executive-order-9981-desegregation-armed-forces.

Library of Virginia. "Brown v. Board of Education: Virginia Responds." 2004. www.lva.virginia.gov.

Cozzens, Lisa. "Early Civil Rights Struggles." 1998. www.watson.org/~lisa/blackhistory/early-civilrights/brown.html.

Orval Faubus

Blackpast. "(1958) Orval E. Faubus, 'Speech on School Integration.'" https://www.blackpast.org/african-american-history/1958-governor-orval-e-faubus-speech-school-integration/.

Rosa Parks

History Learning Site. "Rosa Parks." 2011. https://www.historylearningsite.co.uk/the-civil-rights-movement-in-america-1945-to-1968/rosa-parks/.

RosaParks.com. "Rosa Parks." 2008. https://www.history.com/topics/black-history/rosa-parks.

Jo Ann Robinson

Rivers of Change. "Jo Ann Robinson." N.d. www.riversofchange.org/women_
robinson.html.
African American Registry. "Jo Ann Gibson Robinson, Activist Born." N.d.
https://aaregistry.org/story/jo-ann-gibson-robinson-was-an-unsung-activist/.

Vernon Johns

Momodu, Samuel. "Vernon Napoleon Johns (1892–1965)." BlackPast.org, January
16, 2017. https://www.blackpast.org/african-american-history/johns-vernon-
napoleon-1892-1965/.

Edgar Nixon

Simkin, John. "Edgar Nixon." Spartacus Educational, September 1997. https://
spartacus-educational.com/USACnixon.htm.

Claudette Colvin

Adler, Margot. "Before Rosa Parks, There Was Claudette Colvin." PBS, March 15,
2009. http://www.npr.org/templates/story/story.php?storyId=101719889.

The Montgomery Bus Boycott

Cozzens, Lisa. "Montgomery Bus Boycott." 1997. http://www.watson.org/~lisa/
blackhistory/civilrights-55-65/montbus.html.
King Center. "The Autobiography of Martin Luther King, Jr." 2010. https://
thekingcenter.myshopify.com/collections/by-dr-king-jr.
IPL. "Montgomery Bus Boycott: Civil Rights Movement." N.d. https://www.ipl.
org/essay/Montgomery-Bus-Boycott-Civil-Rights-Movement-FJHQ6ATUZT.

Curtis Harris Jr.

Harris, Curtis, Jr. "The 'Old Days' in Hopewell Weren't So Good for Everyone." Letter to the editor, *Progress-Index*, September 17, 2017. www. progress-index.com/story/opinion/letters/2017/09/20/the-old-days-in-hopewell/18772534007/.

CHAPTER 5

NAACP

History.com Editors. "NAACP." October 29, 2009. https://www.history.com/ topics/civil-rights-movement/naacp.

SCLC

Martin Luther King, Jr. Research and Education Institute. "Southern Christian Leadership Conference (SCLC)." https://kinginstitute.stanford.edu/ encyclopedia/southern-christian-leadership-conference-sclc.

Wayne Tee Walker

Martin Luther King, Jr. Research and Education Institute. "Walker, Wyatt Tee." https://kinginstitute.stanford.edu/encyclopedia/walker-wyatt-tee.

Sit-Ins

Historic Petersburg Foundation. "Historic McKenney Sit-in." Accessed December 18, 2018. http://www.historicpetersburg.org/mckenney-library-sit-in/.
Watson, Denise M. "Lunch Counter Sit-Ins: 50 Years Later." *Virginian Pilot*, February 15, 2010. https://www.pilotonline.com/life/vp-aat-lunch-counter-sitins-50-years-later-20200209-ia6qhzmpmbei3ep3b6suvosdiq-story.html.
Norris, Michele. "The Woolworth Sit-In That Launched a Movement." NPR, February 1, 2008. https://www.npr.org/templates/story/story. php?storyId=18615556.

Southern Regional Council. *The Student Protest Movement: A Recapitulation.* September 29, 1961. https://www.crmvet.org/info/6109_src_sitins.pdf.

King, Martin Luther, Jr. "Statement to the Press at the Beginning of the Youth Leadership Conference." Martin Luther King, Jr. Research and Education Institute. https://kinginstitute.stanford.edu/king-papers/documents/statement-press-beginning-youth-leadership-conference.

Bell v. Maryland

Justia. "Bell v. Maryland, 378 U.S. 226 (1964)." http://supreme.justia.com/us/378/226/.

King in Petersburg

Hamilton Historical Records. "The Beginning Of The Modern Civil Rights Movement In Petersburg, Virginia." https://hamiltonhistoricalrecords.com/2019/03/24/the-beginning-of-the-modern-civil-rights-movement-in-petersburg-virginia/.

Boatwright Commission

"Joseph A. Jordan, Jr., E. A. Dawley, Jr., and L. W. Holt, Appellants, v. J. C. Hutcheson, Chairman, Virginia's Legislative Committee on Offenses Against the Administration of Justice, William King, counsel for the Committee, Honorable Charles Leavitt, City Sergeant, and Committee on Offenses Against the Administration of Justice, Appellees." 323 F.2d 597.

Gilfield Baptist Church

Gilfield Baptist Church. "Gilfield." https://gilfield.com/.

Legal Battles

Edds, Margaret. "Blackballing the Bar." Style Weekly, 2011. https://www.styleweekly.com/richmond/blackballing-the-bar/Content?oid=1378610.

United States Court of Appeals Fourth Circuit. 323 F.2d 597. 1963.

Martin, Howard W., Jr. "Oliver White Hill 1907–2007." Virginia State Bar Association, 2008. http://www.vsb.org/docs/vl1007_president.pdf.

CHAPTER 6

Danville

Gaidmore, Jay. "A Guide to the 1963 Danville (Va.) Civil Rights Case Files, 1963–1973." Library of Virginia, 1999. http://www.lva.virginia.gov/findaid/38099.htm.

Emerge! Magazine. "Dr. Martin Luther King, Jr. in Danville." Spring 2011. https://issuu.com/showcasemagazine/docs/emerge__spring_2011.

Edmunds, Emma C. "Danville Civil Rights Demonstrations of 1963." Encyclopedia Virginia, February 16, 2022. https://www.encyclopediavirginia.org/Danville_Civil_Rights_Demonstrations_of_1963#start_entry.

Birmingham

History Learning Site. "Bull Connor." http://www.historylearningsite.co.uk/bull_connor.htm.

Nunnelley, William. "T. Eugene 'Bull' Connor." Alabama Moments in History. Alabama Department of Archives and History, 1991. http://www.alabamamoments.state.al.us/sec62.html.

University of Alabama Press. "Bull Connor by William A. Nunnelley." http://www.uapress.ua.edu/product/Bull-Connor,463.aspx.

Washington University. "Interview with Wyatt Tee Walker." October 11, 1985. http://digital.wustl.edu/e/eop/eopweb/wal0015.0843.105wyattteewalker.html.

Shuttlesworth

Nordheimer, Jon. "Rev. Fred L. Shuttlesworth, an Elder Statesman for Civil Rights, Dies at 89." *New York Times*, October 5, 2011. https://www.nytimes.com/2011/10/06/us/rev-fred-l-shuttlesworth-civil-rights-leader-dies-at-89.html.

King Letter

Opinio Juris. "Martin Luther King and Civil Disobedience." 2006. www.opiniojuris.org.

March on Washington

Martin Luther King, Jr. Research and Educational Institute. "March on Washington for Jobs and Freedom." https://kinginstitute.stanford.edu/encyclopedia/march-washington-jobs-and-freedom.

Kindig, Jessie. "March on Washington for Jobs and Freedom (August 28, 1963)." BlackPast, December 11, 2007. http://www.blackpast.org/?q=aah/march-washington-jobs-and-freedom-august-28-1963.

National Archives. "Official Program for the March on Washington." Government Documents. U.S. Government, 1996. http://www.ourdocuments.gov/doc.php?flash=true&doc=96.

NPR. "Going to the March." 2003. https://legacy.npr.org/news/specials/march40th/part2.html.

Civil Rights Act

Spartacus Educational. "1964 Civil Rights Act." https://spartacus-educational.com/USAcivilrights.htm.

U.S. Diplomatic Mission to Germany: About the USA. "Speeches by John F. Kennedy: Civil Rights." usa.usembassy.de/etexts/speeches/rhetoric/jfkcivil.htm.

Jimmie Lee Jackson

Spigner, Clarence. "Jimmie Lee Jackson." Encyclopedia of Alabama, January 22, 2009. http://www.encyclopediaofalabama.org/face/Article.jsp?id=h-2011.

Martin Luther King, Jr. Research and Educational Institute. "Jackson, Jimmie Lee." https://kinginstitute.stanford.edu/encyclopedia/jackson-jimmie-lee.

Montgomery March

PBS. "Selma March." 2000. http://www.pbs.org/wgbh/amex/wallace/peopleevents/pande08.html.

Thornton, J. Mills, III. "Selma to Montgomery March." Encyclopedia of Alabama, 2010. http://www.encyclopediaofalabama.org/face/Article.jsp?id=h-1114.

Reed, Roy. "Alabama Police Use Gas and Clubs to Rout Negroes." *New York Times*, 2010. https://www.nytimes.com/1965/03/08/archives/alabama-police-use-gas-and-clubs-to-rout-negroes-57-are-injured-at.html.

Frank M. Johnson Jr.

Bass, Jack. "Frank M. Johnson Jr." Encyclopedia of Alabama, July 26, 2007. http://encyclopediaofalabama.org/article/h-1253.
Academy of Achievement. "Frank M. Johnson, Jr." Last updated March 31, 2022. http://www.achievement.org/autodoc/page/joh2bio-1.

Desegregation of Hopewell

Reuben L. and Joy T. Gilliam

Renee Patrice Gilliam and Reuben Lemuel Gilliam, Jr., Infants, by Reuben L. Gilliam and Joy T. Gilliam, Their Father and Mother and Next Friends, and All Others of the Plaintiffs, Appellants, v. School Board of the City of Hopewell, Virginia, and Charles W. Smith, Division Superintendent of Schools of the City of Hopewell, Virginia, Appellees (two Cases), 345 F.2d 325 (4th Cir. 1965). https://law.justia.com/cases/federal/appellate-courts/F2/345/325/327882/.

CHAPTER 7

Senator Henry Marsh

Poff, Marietta Elizabeth. "School Desegregation in Roanoke, Virginia: The Black Student Perspective." PhD diss., Virginia Tech, 2014. https://vtechworks.lib.vt.edu/bitstream/handle/10919/56661/Poff_ME_D_2014.pdf.

Governor J. Lindsay Almond

Library of Virginia. "Virginians Respond to the Decision and Aftermath: A Collection of Library of Virginia Documents." https://www.lva.virginia.gov/exhibits/brown/browndocs.htm.

Resurrection City on the Mall

Diamond, Anna. "Remembering Resurrection City and the Poor People's Campaign of 1968." *Smithsonian Magazine* 408 (May 2018). https://www.smithsonianmag.com/history/remembering-poor-peoples-campaign-180968742/.

Heppermann, Ann, and Kara Oehler. "This Weekend in 1968: The Legacy of Resurrection City." American Public Media, 2008. http://weekendamerica.publicradio.org/display/web/2008/05/08/1968_resurrection/.

State Senator Garland "Peck" Gray

TIME. "Virginia Creeper." January 2, 1956. http://www.time.com/time/magazine/article/0,9171,808079,00.html.

Dupont, Carolyn. "Race, Reason, and Massive Resistance: The Diary of David J. Mays, 1954–1959." *Journal of Southern History* (2009). http://findarticles.com/p/articles/mi_hb6532/is_3_75/ai_n35542557/.

Colonial Heights

Baker, Donald P. "SCLC Plans to March in Colonial Heights, VA." *Washington Post*, March 29, 1987. https://www.washingtonpost.com/archive/local/1987/03/29/sclc-plans-to-march-in-colonial-heights-va/ee2d9d17-f98a-4032-ba63-fdc49685855f/.

Melton, R.H. "White Separatists March in Colonial Heights, VA." *Washington Post*, April 12, 1987. https://www.washingtonpost.com/archive/local/1987/04/12/white-separatists-march-in-colonial-heights-va/433c4c49-f729-4e63-a641-417079d85183.

Williamsburg Slave Auction

Eggan, Dan. "In Williamsburg, the Painful Reality of Slavery " *Washington Post*, July 7, 1999. http://www.washingtonpost.com/wp-srv/local/daily/july99/williamsburg7.htm.

Baltimore Sun. "'Slave Auction' Divides Crowd in Williamsburg." 1994. http://articles.baltimoresun.com/1994-10-11/news/1994284095_1_williamsburg-foundation-colonial-williamsburg-slave-auction.

Ethanol Plant

Bell, Nicole. "Equipment Failure Blamed for Ethanol Plant Explosion in Hopewell." NBC-12, September 10, 2010. http://www.nbc12.com/story/13128231/equipment-failure-blamed-for-ethanol-plant-explosion-in-hopewell.

Andrew Shannon

Reyes, Josh. "Civil Rights Icon Remembered for Decades Long Commitment." *Daily Press*, Newport News, VA December 18, 2017. https://www.dailypress.com/government/dp-nws-curtis-harris-civil-rights-20171217-story.html.

Interviews with the Reverend Curtis West Harris Sr.

University of Florida, George M. Smathers Library. "Interview with Rev. Curtis W. Harris, February 27, 2003." http://ufdc.ufl.edu/UF00093253/00001.
Carrington, Ronald E. "Interview with Rev. Curtis W. Harris." Voices of Freedom. Virginia Commonwealth University, 2003. https://digital.library.vcu.edu/islandora/object/vcu:38562.
Lee, Lauranett L. *Making the American Dream Work: A Cultural History of African Americans in Hopewell, Virginia.* New York: Morgan James Publishing, 2008.
Ragsdale, Ben. "A Higher Law: Rev. Curtis Harris." 2017. http://www.curtiswharris.com/commentary.html

INDEX

ABOUT THE AUTHOR

William Paul Lazarus is an award-winning newspaper reporter and magazine editor who has published a variety of fiction and nonfiction books on a wide array of topics, including *A Guide to American Culture* and *Passover in Prison: Abuses and Challenges Faced by Jews in America's Prisons*. He holds an ABD in American studies from Case Western Reserve University (Ohio) and has taught at various colleges and universities, including Yale, Kent State University (Ohio), the University of New Haven (Connecticut), Embry-Riddle Aeronautical University (Florida) and Daytona State College (Florida). His books are sold worldwide and can be found on Amazon.com, Kindle.com and other sites.